NEW
&
SELECTED
POEMS

Copyright: Andrew Burke 2020

This book is copyright. Apart from any fair dealing for the purposes of study and research, criticism, review, or as otherwise permitted under the Copyright Act, no part may be reproduced in any manner without first gaining written permission from the author.

Walleah Press
5/23 Cross Street
New Town
Tasmania 7008 Australia
ralph.wessman@walleahpress.com.au

ISBN: 978-1-877010-95-8

Walleah Press

NEW & SELECTED POEMS

ANDREW BURKE

Copyright 2020

Biographical Note

Andrew Burke is an Australian poet who has lived most of his life in Perth. After his birth in Melbourne in 1944, Burke's family moved west to expand the family business. In his teens, Burke read 'Beat' writers, and they gained his interest more than school work. He published his first short story at 18. He has written on a daily basis ever since – stories, plays, poems, and – to feed family – advertising material and videos. From 1990, Burke taught creative writing and modern literature at universities, TAFE colleges and writing centres. In 2006, he and his wife Jeanette travelled to China where they taught at Shanxi Normal University, Linfen, and, on their return, they taught indigenous children in the Kimberley area of North West Australia. He now dedicates life fulltime to reading and writing.

Other Books by Andrew Burke

Let's Face the Music & Dance 1973
On the Tip of my Tongue 1982
Mother Waits for Father Late 1992
Pushing at Silence 1996
Whispering Gallery 2001
Knock on Wood 2003
Beyond City Limits 2009
Mother Waits for Father Late – Revised 2010
E-Novel: Blue Rose
{QWERTY} take my word for it 2011
Shikibu Shuffle 2012
Undercover of Lightness: New & Selected 2012
One Hour Seeds Another 2014
The Line is Busy 2017

CONTENTS

Ars Poetica 1

Withered Garden 3
Running Fig 5
Climbing Kelly's Knob 6
North West Flight 8
Frogs and Rocks border the Southern Ocean 11
Occupation Folding Bags 12
Dwellingup Smokes 13
April Jazz Poem 15
Sitting Together 16
Sitting Alone 17
Bananas 18
New Spiders 19
Song for the New Born 20
Nightmare 21
Poems for Julia 22
After You've Gone 25
Where I Live 26
Dream Song 27
Room Service 28
Making Love at Mary's 29
Whitebait 30
Father 31
Mother Waits for Father Late 32
Dear Father 35
More Booze 36
Sunday Roast 37
Diary of a Bad Back 39
Elegy for My Mother 42
Birthday Angels 43

Hallway Chair at Mothers   44
Angels for Charlie   45
Third Step   46
Owl on Caddy's Farm   47
Peaceful Bay   48
On the Road to Denmark   52
Along the Tideline   54
Melros Beach   56
Elegance   57
Poetry Housekeeping   58
Whale's Ear in a Country Museum   59
The Pianoless Quartet   60
Mary Anne at Kookynie   61
None so Raw as This Our Land   62
Natural SFX   63
Esse Est Percipi   65
Autobiography   66
Sharp-smelling Mist   67
Mr Hobby's Poppies   69
The Perfume Factory   70
Testament   71
The Rosary Beads   76
Little White Pills   77
Walking to the Meeting   78
The Kid's Last Fight   80
The Present Depression   82
Rainy Days   83
A Ceremony of Sorts   84
The Old Tambourine   85
Simple Truth Meditation   86
Mandala Wok   87
Regional Aeolian   88
The God Bottle   89

As We Are   90
Going Home   91
Shop Locally   93
Shopping Centre Genius   94
Have a Nice Day   95
Snap Dragon   97
Apologia   98
Factory Life   99
The Ophthalmic Prosthetist   100
for days I have watched in wonder   101
On the Third Day   102
On Chapman Hill   103
Details   104
Dorothy Dorothy Dorothy   105
Writing on a Brown Bag in Freo   106
the limits of my language are the limits of my world   108
Bad Weather   109
Paddler   110
Washing   112
Washing Day   113
A Day in the Life   114
Diary RPH 2010   115
Home from Hospital   121
Unfold   122
Upside-down Sonnet   123
Bike Mechanics   124
Linfen Morning   126
More Rain Today   127
'Teaching now'   128
Manhole Covers   129
Epistle to Andrew Taylor   130
The Clean Air Act of 1956   132
Snow in Linfen   133

Tai Bai Mountain   134
Linfen Taxi Ride   135
Raw   137
The Next Poem   138
Shining to the Misty Hills   139
Spice of Life   140
Tootle Lingo   141
Happy Hour   142
Gibb River Rip Rap   143
Gibb River Yacht Club   144
Ngallagunda Used Car Yard   145
Ngallagunda Girl   146
Grooves   147
The adventure novel of everyday life   148
Water Colour Morning   150
The Ballad of Many Crows   151
The Best Teacher   153
The Name of the Game   154
Notebook: Singing They Sang   156
Sitting on the Front Perch   159
Notebook: Darlington   160
Late Winter Night   161
On the Verge   162
Counting the Beads   164
If the World is Thought   165
Chainman in Summer   168
The birds are still in flight. Believe the birds.   169
Anaesthetics   170
Under a Black Beret   172
Self-portrait with Bee   173
The Other Woman   174
Love, Oh Love, Oh Careless Love   175
She Waits for Me   176
I Remember Lucas   177

NEW POEMS

Absence   178
Aneurysm   179
XPT Sydney to Melbourne   181
Local Language   185
Notebook: Cafe Poem   186
Moody Requiem   187
The Wheelie Bin Novel   188
Reverse Haibun   189
Paper Tales   190
At Woolies' Car Park   191
Playing a 500 Year-Old Oak   192
Echidna Crossing   194
Spring Silence   195
Afternoon Tea   196

ACKNOWLEDGEMENTS

Thanks are due to the numerous editors and publishers of the various magazines, newspapers and anthologies in which these poems first appeared.

In the process of putting this book together I have had the wonderful editorial advice and friendship of David Brooks, Andrew Taylor and Geoff Page. The selection was also ably supported by Delryne Sherrett and a little writing group comprising of Jayne Surrey, Rob Rose and Patrick Speed – I thank them all.

My long-term mate Murray Jennings also had a say in this – thanks for all the years of friendship, music advice and poetry conversations.

For the wondrous freehand calligraphy on the cover, I am honoured to thank for grand daughter, Sophie Bahiyyih Jain. What life it brings to over-used words!

I have always wanted a consistent publisher for my poetry – a deep-seated clan impulse, I suppose – so I am extremely happy to be published again by Ralph Wessman at Walleah Press in Hobart, Tasmania. Ralph and his partner Jane Williams are long time supporters of Australian poetry and so I thank them for their work and their friendship.

Lastly I would like to thank my wife Jeanette Margaret Burke who has read many of these poems in 'first draft' mode and made criticisms where they were needed.

In the NEW POEMS thanks are due to the Editors of *Oz Burp* (Pete Spence), *Best Australian Poems 2015* (Geoff Page), *Shot from the Chamber* (anthol. Myron Lysenko et al.), *The Mozzie* (Ron Heard), *Australian Poetry Anthology Vol. 7 2019* (Yvette Holt & Magan Magan), *Communion Arts Journal* (Jane Williams).

Ah, so many people along the track to thank! Thanks for all the readers, critics and students who have responded to my poetry in any way.

With gratitude to
TOM SHAPCOTT
Poet and Teacher

ARS POETICA

My heart is still beating –
it jumped a beat when
my first cry
startled the surgeon.
Now I'm still trying
to translate it –
sound before music,
beat before language.

I'll wake in the morning,
in the tail spin of a dream
– and prepare breakfast:
grind coffee beans,
toast bread, whip
eggs into a scramble

whistling kettle
grinding beans
hiss of gas when it
first flares – all will be
in any poem I write today:
sound before music,
beat before language.

from *Let's Face the Music and Dance*

THE WITHERED GARDEN

the lawn lies scarred
beneath the savage sun.
the beer bottle lies
too hot to handle –
i emptied it last night,
looking the moon
full in the face,
listening to the tin shed
rattle on its loose nails.

between the withered garden
and her adrift again
from my bobbing buoy,
i gasp for meaning
        as the plastic container
                contorts, then
      flows in
our dustbin on fire.

a)

we've just come out of the doctor's
"It is for you, you two,
      to decide. I
          simply present possibilities."

we walk out and down the road …

"well, what do you think?"
and i am thinking of the bus
and where the stop is
and if we have the fare
      when a tomato bush
      catches my eye
growing amongst
the fresh pebbles
of a parking lot.

b)

the potato mound
is a child's grave and
buries my hope. the image
collapses the tent. i
return to bed. we lie
like beetles
on our backs

from *On the Tip of My Tongue*

RUNNING FIG
(for TW Shapcott)

'It is a kind of running fig
grown for its juvenile leaf –
there, on the stone,
that's the young plant.
This long-armed big-leaf overspill
is the adult.
Once it gets to this stage
it'll run away … '
He chops with his hands
at the end of
four hours editing:
'It depends what you like
but you could
cut it back.'

from *Flight Log*

CLIMBING KELLY'S KNOB

Climbing Kelly's Knob
                    knobs like waves
about to break on the shore –
                          broken beer bottles
                        rusty cans
                              crow calls
the hawks circle forever
                        sandstone breaking up
        layer on layer …

At Hidden Valley
            the aborigines' 'land of dreaming'
boabs like wine bottles
                  Hidden Valley
'formed 300,000,000 years ago under the sea'
                                    tall sides
fallen lumps
            creek flows through in the wet
                      roos eat the fresh
greens.

A hollow in the rockface
                  like a holy shrine
no St Theresa or Mother Mary or Joseph –
                            and no Buddha
sitting in the bus
            in the shade of centuries.

Yellow wildflowers on thin trees
                        dead fruit bat with vampire fangs
     at a boab's foot ...

Aborigines rubbed their spears sharp
                        on these rocks
their grooves still here ...
                        and sitting in all this history
a polite white shed.
               water lilies on the backflow of Lake Argyle
                       a brolga
                               in the silt ...

NORTHWEST FLIGHT

Gum Tree Valley
            Aboriginal paintings
100 to 25,000 years old –
            small mountains
topped with dark chocolate rocks – jabaroos about –
colonies of herons and ibis – euros galore.

Seashells show the campsite –
            aboriginal seafood feasts
           through centuries
stopping to do and redo the sacred drawings –
shells show age and what season eaten –
           identifying what the sea level was doing.

Carvings :: fish   goanna   kadarchi man (carved and
           over carved deep into time)
handshapes   gigantic genitalia
    man like a tripod   woman swollen labia like balls

On the road's crest
           our art for safety's
                      sake.

White ants draw a black stripe down the dead gum
sheltering from the sun.

Euro shit by the fresh water hole.

Layered shells   silent calendar of the past.

*

Driving back slow clouds over the mountains
overlooking Dampier Archipelago –
                          above the high school
     a kite
          with an eagle
painted on it.

Dampier Port Control
               a space ship
                         on the hill
on the horizon
          six tankers await word.

Rocks so high in 'fe' –
               69% to 72% -
                             you could weld
two rocks together!

Dampier workman '$40,000 house for $10 a week –
               Hard to take, eh?' Grin.

*

Off again into
          black syrup night –
moon hangs
               chewed fingernail
                        of a moon.

*

The spirit of Newman –
               singing chanting
               dancing group *You'll be back!*

        they scream to their friends,
                              leaving.
        They say it with such conviction
        you know the leavers will never return
        except in Social Club slides
        on the Recreation Club wall.

The chorus crows at dawn
                Monday morning
bleak motel backyard ...
up the bathroom wall
a gecko
        fast as a flash
suckles on its feet ...

        Last town on the last day.
        Sad and tired
                the Mullaya Leprosy Mission truck
                lies under a gum.

*

Opthalmia Range into the Kimberley –
dust brown bird like a sparrow
                          gone mining –
giant shovels cost $2.2 million!
What did Stand Hilditch dig with
when he discovered uncovered this wealth?
Biggest opencut iron ore mine in the world ...

'It'll be greener than when we began
When we leave in about 34 years ...'
                          PRO said that ...

FROGS AND ROCKS BORDER THE SOUTHERN OCEAN

Peaceful Bay.
The frogs speak the same tongue
as the rocks :: changelessness.
It's in opposition to the facts
but facts are not all there is
after all – timeless tongues
lap here in the ocean's grammar book.
We cart books in an overstuffed car
to return them unread   We read
tongues in rock, ocean, bird, frog –
bound by time   hardbacked by nature.

OCCUPATION : FOLDING BAGS

Possibly in his dreams he's whole
Straight-eyed straight body   in control
Captain of himself from each dawn –
And you would have him not born
For his maladies?!
His head will fall off!
But the spirit in his lurching gait
Is his return weight.

He folds bags.
With his elbows he clubs them
in a centre-fold smooth action,
he turns
and folds again and again –
Fat Annie can't make her bags that flat!
Cop that! and his laugh
ruins the next fold.
He clubs the bench,
goddamn goddamn ...

He leaves –
the traffic halts
as he
lurches across the highway
like a
wilful puppet.
The busdriver demands his pension pass.
He slaps his coat   big pockets flap
Where is it?! Where is it?!
The pass! Here, driver, drive on –
he's captain again,
in control.

DWELLINGUP SMOKES

Distant mill smoke
signals 'town ahead'.
We drive towards it
in our different smokes:
car fumes   tobacco smokes
smoking roadside logs –
our bodies burning,
         exhaust breaths…
All trees –
        pine
        banksia
        gum –
doing their job on the air,
breathing out.

i

Dwellingup Railway Station
brilliant sunshine yellow
full gloss in the rain.
The town is ringbarked –
Forestry Commission
cut back
on cutting timber
so
the town falls.

ii

Green hills border
the road out of town
far hills grey. A
bone-white tree stands
straight-up
to surprise the landscape.

iii

Cows
after rain
stand like
wet farmhouse rugs
flung over bushes
to dry.

iv

This road
once trail
dictated by
farm boundaries
its quirky syntax
yesterday's work-of-man
we use today,
driving A to B
through history.

Animal habits
prompt my song,
doing my job,
singing.

APRIL JAZZ POEM

Ben Webster is playing
love songs inside me
and you've thrown your hair
back into his luscious wet runs
coming straight up the beach
where we are dancing,
dancing in the dunes –
it's some kind of moonlit ballroom
where we are dancing
love songs inside me.

from *Mother Waits for Father Late (1992)*

SITTING TOGETHER

There are prayers
that rise
from our wind chimes

as we sit
together
in veranda shade

smoke rises
from the hills
around us

Alice cannot keep
all her songs
inside her

So she gently hums
not to interrupt
our worrying

SITTING ALONE

In this
blistering heat
I sit alone

dog's hot breath
on my bare feet
house silent

only the distant
pool filter hums

seeds are coming
alive in the earth
eggs cracking

all my unwritten
poems are rising
to be born

BANANAS
for Tom Shapcott

You can't exercise on this fruit
despite its distant relationship
with monkey bars. It is bent phallic,
a late night disappointment after
the bar and all for the girl who
peeled her catsuit off like
another skin to let you in. You
were a soft, over-ripe appointment,
follied further by limp promises,
'next time'. . . As if. You hugged
the metaphor in the taxi home,
then slept on it, monkish.

NEW SPIDERS

In the bathroom's musty shadows
eggs have hatched
many little spiders rock the web
uncertain   just whose reality
is theirs

Legs wobbly   I crouch and stare

Take care spiders   he who kills ants
will wake soon   he will not hesitate
to spray and squash you   Sure he will
talk to you   as I do but he is
young and does not understand
life's fragility

         Precognizance
of Buddha's word is a tenuous web
to cling to

SONG FOR THE NEWBORN
for Jessica Brooks

In the dark hours
you bring myths
to songs

in a tongue
before time
where you have just been

Every time you remember
timelessness it slips
away like a favourite song

You sing it back
to dream's border
but we stopper your mouth

Listen how your
dawn birds
sing

Now   sing back

NIGHTMARE

Time takes different corners
in the dark

I was holding my baby son
he was smiling and I
hugged him   something fell
out of his mouth   I picked it
off his bib   it was his tongue
Fear froze me   I lost my tongue
grunted in fear   snorted holding it
my head thrashing   his face
smiling   his tongueless mouth open
as a cave
His tongue had come out
bloodless and warm like fish
from the river – I stood
tongue in one hand
songless baby in the other

I wanted to wrap the tongue in a towel
but I couldn't move   speechless I couldn't
cry out   he should have cried out
his mother would have come if he had cried out
He was smiling at me   thrashing my head
fitfully holding his tongue

I wake and sweat
I flick my tongue and hear
   frogs in
      the first autumn rain

POEMS FOR JULIA

1)

Paper lies
covering
the peninsulas

of dry words, a tongue
extended …
Pleas of time lick by. –

Paperlight stands up
moving
through eyes like music –

windy night
waves
ghost flags –

paperlight shrinks
back
 to the page.

Radio crackles on
saying 'I conclude',
transubstantiating

ii)

In the closely guarded ward
sun stops
at the receptionist's feet
An orderly let me in –
no gimmicks or fancy gifts –
just me   after work
on impulse. I caught you wigless
four days grey growth
topping your round
flushed face –
your hand flew
to tidy lost hair.

Across our lifetime aloofness
we kissed   your lips
tasted sweet

My last time with you
remains

iii)

You pedal me
fast to preschool before I
wet my dinkyseat

pedal fast over
rolling greens

*'what will the nuns say
if he wets his pants?'*

convent skirt and straw hat
dance in front of me

as you pedal fast
fast as you can

with your friends making a game of it
to keep all our respects

Tonight the peacock's
harsh bark
brings me to ground.

Your grey hair will grow
beneath earth tomorrow
fine as grass roots

birds will fly
in your light voice
as almond blossom falls —

white silence

To bury you we will
sing, kneel and pray.

I will bring roses
for their discipline,
 a homegrown rosary.

AFTER YOU'VE GONE
for Ray

Crows sang   at your funeral
a gratuitous song   pines
dripped tears
of grief   of rage
Our sister made a bad joke.   I
looked away

to see two rosellas walking
fronds on a giant palm:
all so calm
I walked home   grave sand
in hand   wet rain.
  Because

you were buried Catholic
you have Italian neighbours,
a sprinkler
at your feet   How do
such facts rest in Heaven?

WHERE I LIVE

Where I live
has a tail of night flowers
that open as I turn,
close when you are near.

I hold you to own you.
You spill into
other lives,
other nights are light with you.

Where I live
is standing still
windless weatherboard sails,
shadowless sands of my heart.

I turn again
to hear
you sing in empty
country halls on tour.
We teach the children their address:

old addresses
wave behind us
old loves   jazz until dawn
attendant psychiatrists and organic gardens.

Here I live
outside the city
planting trees by moonlight
hand immersed in their milk-white roots.

A DREAM SONG
after Berryman

Inconceivably Andrew sang of night
things that ends him up   falls again
so long.
– Easy, Mister Bones, they might
hears you. – Heeds me? Deaf in pain
I am to my true self   my song

a spluttery rubber balloon
down a length of room
damps
her greedless lap. My rising sap?
So much spit. They billed me
seedless   I shoot blanks.

I distress me   every day
born again in dawn's re-
erection
after wreck of night, say,
(sing!), 'the pump don't work
coz the vandals took the handle'

ROOM SERVICE

This quiet morning
I bring you
breakfast in bed:

corn flakes,
coffee,
an orange
nasturtium
on a long stem
in a tiny
'antique' bottle

You say
I am   obvious

MAKING LOVE AT MARY'S

Awake from snoring away
hours of Spring afternoon
we sit reading in the kitchen at Mary's
as waves of jazz piano wash over us
taut strings hit by velvet hammers at
Koln January 1975 bought bootleg
in Bali 1982   re-aired in
Rockingham September 1988
tie our hearts together
measure for contra-
puntal measure   hour
on sunny hour   until
we fall into bed

and romp

WHITE-BAIT

White-bait, those tiniest sliver
of silver words, swim into
my mind from dark nights
when Mother would feed
the surprise guest brought home
by Father with one too many
drinks in him. Many times
they would mumble apologies
while mother speared a tin
of King Sound White-bait
and started toast cooking.
Father brought home
interesting people, men
who had caught his ear
at the yacht club or the
Naval & Military Club:
American film actor,
CSIRO scientist, touring
Italian pianist, war hero
with tin legs. Mother would
heat whitebait slowly in
cream sauce, and when
the toast popped-up (we had
a modern kitchen), she would
say, *Sit down, sit down,*
and all the white-baits' eyes
would look-up at
my father and his guest
swaying like sailors
just come home from sea.

FATHER

i)
Tonight your blood rises to high tide in me
Each second your frog in my wrist jumps
You wake my fear after all these years
I want to talk through your open mouth
I want to close it   Hear me

ii)
Sit down   let's talk
I can't remember one word
you ever said to me
I can't forget your morning needles
the horror of you
puncturing your pinched stomach skinfold
as I lay in my bath before school
shriveled in fear
breath out of rhythm
eyes stinging wide open
I washed and washed
until my navel ached

Every needle I've known since
shoots back the pain

MOTHER WAITS FOR FATHER LATE

Mother sitting at the long kitchen table
bottle and glass and book open but hardly read
waiting for Father who is as always late.

As always late he rolls in – I must have been
asleep upstairs and innocent at nine years – to tell
the bad news he had delayed telling: old lady dead
on Stirling Highway by his car's thump –
'She just walked out into the car, she was old,
just stepped off the curb – My bad luck
she chose me.' He drove to the pub
after police interviews,
to delay the telling of it
but told the boys in the bar well enough.

I was dreaming so who told me? I must have known
early next day before I picked up the phone
to hear a crazy voice say, 'Murderer! Murderer!
You can buy your way out of it this time
but you'll get yours, mate, you'll get yours!'

Weeks later Father lay still in their giant bedroom
drinking crates of Coca-Cola, no way to quench
his thirst: diabetes brought on by shock. Hospital,
tests, new life programme, insulin shots
morning and night. not too much sun, no boozing,
watch that diet. Impossible. The wittiest man
at The Naval and Military Club, soul of the party
at Freshwater Bay Yacht Club, backbone
of 'the Killing Pen' at Steve McHenry's famous pub,
he could not change his habits overnight. So

comas came on. Mother and I forcing sugar in water
down his throat, one on each side of the bed,
passing the glass across hurriedly as he
rolled, getting it into him
for his life's sake.
His brothers flew across Australia to his hospital bed
to force him out of their rich company. He signed.
Pride would not let him fight them off or ask
for help. Doomed by guilt, trapped
by alcohol, sick and tired, he went to bed
yet one more time. This night jelly bowls of blood
jumped out, Mother sick herself on the couch,
I called the doctor. Mother and I rode
in the ambulance, sat in cold hospital corridors
frightened of death. Caught a taxi home.
Driver kept Mother downstairs
while I cleaned Father's blood off their bedroom floor
as best I could. My fourteenth birthday. He died
two weeks later. My sick mind cleaned up
as best it could
                until, wacked on
booze and dope, that night rose again
fifteen years later and drove me
to a cliff's edge where I aimed at the sky.
My car bogged and I ran
to that doctor's house, vomited over him
as he opened the door, 5am, startled.

I woke in hospital. White bed, white walls, blue river
through green pine trees out my window, worried
wife and child at home. I stared, wondering who was I,
asked my tidy shrink for LSD, I wanted it all to rise,
to know the sweetness and horror of all my days.
He controlled me on pills and platitudes.

Photos show a happy man, young wife and son, dressed
Seventies style, fit, smiling, curator
of a writers' cottage by the ocean, where
the music of Dylan and Zappa mingled with Miles Davis
beyond the sound of colonial banjos.

Eight months later, dressed in white,
daisychains around our necks and in our hair,
we drove at dawn to
an artist's champagne breakfast in the hills,
giant trees in the yard, minimalist paintings on the walls.
In my mood even eggs-and-bacon looked bohemian
as I drank orange juice, champagne-and-orange,
champagne, then whatever
alcohol I could find… Made my usual Jesus jokes
about turning water into wine, wine into water. Spent
late afternoon attempting to blow up petrol stations across
the escarpment with strips of cloth alight, laughing
uncontrollably at who knows what.

Blackouts returned, fights, lost days of
fear and loathing, my combatant driving … I swung
an axe at my love's neck, went to lunch Friday
came home Sunday, not knowing where I'd been,
who I'd seen, days of life lost. With me late as usual,
wife gave up waiting, locked our windows and doors.

I slept black nights in a ratty tin shed.

DEAR FATHER

How sick I get of your ghost
stirring the blood between us,
how sick of the ties
that hold me.

Father, a shrink on the highway
told me to write. To who?
I have made you up. You are
the air in my birthday balloon
the clown at our barbecue
proud patron of the bottle-o
you shape my fingers and my toes
you cast my shadow
my every look over the shoulder
you carve my tombstone in womb bone.

How sick I get of my ties to you.
Let this be a letter
to the Dead Letter Office.
(I'm sick of your jokes.)

Father, I untie you –
air rushes out
and I whoop…

I'm fifty,
it's time to let go.

MORE BOOZE

Looking to buy more booze
we cut open the moneybox
that's a Big Red Boomer.
The children count the coins:
their education could be worse.
In the kitchen we total up
empties. The morning sun
rises to the occasion. Our days
keep their change close. Puns
come soon, then, in
the afternoon, sullen
evening drops in, early.

SUNDAY ROAST

In this room I surround myself
with books
open like birds in flight

Through my door a smell
of roast
takes me back to childhood

brothers and sisters and I
roamed the house
asking Mother for lunch

as roast potatoes spat
oven door
opened and slammed

gravy's deep brown consistency
stirred with
a flat wooden spoon

Six streets away at Freshwater Bay
Yacht Club
Father stood 'just one more

for the road'. Oven was
turned down
afternoon grumbled on

pale-faced plates on the table
knives and forks
straightened again and again

I still have the iron
Father flailed
his carving knife at

in a swashbuckling rhythm which
called us
to lunch 3.45 Sunday

Today I hunger for us
to be
impossibly together again

I close my books and go
walking
this grey day in Spring.

DIARY OF A BAD BACK
for my mother

From the library
I borrow 'The End of Senility'
thinking of you
forgetting all the time lately
how you worry about it
so much
it makes forgetting worse ...

or am I
foolishly
trying to tie the clock's hands
behind its back?

*

At the doctor's surgery
when they ask you
your birth year
you turn to me as if I'd know
'1912? 1913?'
History book years to me
'Oh, you know ...'

I know
you let your cat eat
better than you
and report on his health
before your own

I say
you forget *yourself* too much

I wonder
where your piano is now?
Who is learning scales
on your last upright
left in Melbourne
in nineteen forty what?

*

Today your back is worse
you phone to say
you cried this morning

This pre-mourning is
mixed with
pointless anger

a ragbag
of emotions
tossed in despair

*

Again you ring
your back is worse

'Please buy catfood and milk ...'

I go   I buy   I return
the phone is ringing

You have just rung to say
don't bother
you looked in the fridge
there's enough

You are feeling
so much better now
the cat has eaten

*

X-rays show
your spine is thin
and fractured

Each step
up your stairs
is a new pain

My ragbag is torn

I turn away
and see
my children

waiting
on the first stair

ELEGY FOR MY MOTHER
Hilda Mary Burke 1912-93

Two with sympathy cards today
among our cheery Christmas mail.
My mother died last Tuesday –

a mixed blessing the nurses say.
Mixed? Yes, she had grown so frail.
Two 'With Sympathy' cards today –

some must read that list each day.
Death danced across our trail
when Mother died last Tuesday.

At her wake there was much to say
about sport, weather and local ale.
Two "With Sympathy' cards today –

now the undertaker wants his pay.
Behind a cloud the moon is pale.
My mother died last Tuesday.

A mixed blessing, so they say:
God's daughter's death, a nativity tale.
Two 'With Sympathy' cards today,
my mother died last Tuesday.

BIRTHDAY ANGELS

My childhood favourite
was a heavy black
wooden chair

stumpy carved legs
stood on lion paws
holding their ground

around the flat seat
a hardwood hem
with indented archways

Each birthday
I knocked on
an archway door

seven for my seventh
eight for my eighth

asking a blessing
of my birthday angel

Head propped on hands
I waited   elbows bent
by the lion paws

HALLWAY CHAIR AT MOTHER'S

Every time I arrive   at Mother's
too long between visits   I run
my hands over   the hallway chair's
round back   to feel the smoothness of
generations of family   to know
the seat of   hot bodies running in
from summer games   or cold
bodies wet   from heaven's rain

all of us   come home

ANGELS FOR CHARLIE

Angels are in you
wings open
to embrace the start of day
Angels lift bones
from your bag
of dreams
interconnecting
all working parts
and walk you
to breakfast half awake –
who else pours
the milk? spreads
the jam?

THIRD STEP
'Made a decision to turn our will and our lives over to
the care of God as we understood Him'
(from the Twelve Steps of Alcoholics Anonymous)

Bread and wine into
body and blood
each priest's daily duty

fingers crocked holding
Christ aloft
like circus jugglers

Sober three months
I searched
for my love of God

In Darlington's cracked
stone church
I recoiled from wine

switched to Sawyer's Valley
Christian Fellowship
where Christ's blood came

in glass thimbles
fresh grape juice
pure and simple

Now ten years sober
this bread and water way
God holds my will

in trust:
He downs my ups
and ups my downs

Every day I wake
I give
my will away

OWL ON CADDY'S FARM

On the farmhouse wall
                         hangs
          Caroline's drawing of owl
feathers closed
               wings awkward
      from fall...
                 he is
      image of a tree bough
body
         living woodiness
                texture
      look of bark
graphite shadings
          his eyes
                 see fields
       map the Blackwood River
 where it dams
and elbows its way
            through trees

He eats mince
with a piece of loving heart
cut feather as roughage

         *

        Three yellow stones
             dug out of earth
     are stepping stones to the pond where
a moonlit tantric spot
grows in moss

Owl's mind
     owns this place

PEACEFUL BAY

Two hours down Highway 1
breakfast by roadside

coffee steam
    mingles
      with morning mist

Donnybrook at dawn

    we take it in turns
    to piss
    in an empty lot
    off Main Street

*

Mist hangs so heavy
road gets lost

headlights cut through
hill hollows of fog

soup in a bowl

*

We arrive   Peaceful Bay is ripped
by power saws   loud mowers
    cut scrappy lawns   trim edges
owners spend their time
    upkeeping shacks   fishing
      getting pissed

    Teenage dudes suck on stubbies
        drive panel vans
            customized   flash

Harold   monochromatic dog
      yaps dawn to dusk
           happy to be here

*

'Come an' have a drink –
got ya stubby holder?'

*

Lonesome kid kicks a footy
on pebbly 3rd Avenue
(streets named the New York way!)

Thong flies with the ball
      like a bird
following its mother close

Peppermint tree takes a high mark
kid yells 'What a beauty!'

*

Mushrooms!

We search wet-with-dew-at-noon kikuya grass
lifting an upturned wormholed wooden chest—
      yellow grass beneath
          shrinks back
              surprised—
not one.

Not surprised.
*

'Coffee or tea?'
Tea or coffee?'

'Toffee, thanks.'
'Only got honeycomb.'

*

Two peppermints grow out of an old banksia
      translucent pink fingers on red hands

old tree wears a moss shawl
      around hunched stony shoulders

*

Elders of the tribe talk over a ute tray
stubbies in their hands
sons wear footy guernseys   maroon-&-gold
      black-&-white ... stubby holders
carry club emblems   The Lions   The Tigers
      the roar of the crowd
fills their silences ...

Genesis :: the Family Tree   Pop builds here
son builds there
              grandson too young
for footy on 3rd Avenue   watches
         itchy in his thongs   shadowing the play

Smoke flies between shacks   little Meg
         in dusty green Speedo bathers
runs up the pebbly road   slipping
         carrying her dog   pleading
'He's hurt! He's hurt!'

Harold looks amazed   juggled ragtoy

*

Community Noticeboard message:
         'Sharon – Crain not coming today'
spelling out what is set

*

In the dunes   ants build a dome
of tiny dry sticks ...
no contract to sign
no shire orders
they build their city
singing with activity

ON THE ROAD TO DENMARK

Cows sit on
a dam's ridge
like toys from
a farmyard pack

Big rock mountains
grow out of Earth
like cracked
museum skulls
wrapped tightly to
distend for fashion:

landscape's
old grey brain

*

Denmark Easter Saturday Market:

'Old Tyres Turned Into Beauty'
cut and turned inside out
and round-about
as swans

painted white with
original tyre-black
showing through
in dramatic effect.

We stop and stare.
Children run crazily
caught in Autumn's crossfire
leaves drifting down

*

Straight road
rises   falls
like a slow
sideshow alley
ride

NEW WORK
NO LINES
MARKED

Everyone writes poems
driving to Denmark
inspired

ALONG THE TIDELINE

fifty snub-nosed old tractors line up—Duffields,
    Massey Harrises, Massey Fergusons, Nelson &
    Browns—rusty trailers like red tails pointing
    out to sea up and down the beach barking
    kelpies run, crazed by ocean smells and teasing
    seagulls . women knit seaweed scarves, talking
    with fish mouths and pink tongues . fat men
    jostle with jellyfish bellies, dribbling beer from
    stubbies cooled in rusting Eskys

seagulls stand strong, facing the wind on the rocks
    above the reef that points into the bay . Mother
    Dog pisses and a rusty stain runs to the South
    Pole

aluminium Noah's Ark hoves into view : two metres
    long, small Evinrude outboard at back . Noah
    wears old khaki army jumper, floppy sunhat,
    faded baggy Hawaiian bathers . today Missus
    Noah wears a yellow oilskin, her grey hair in a
    permanent wave

Southern Ocean runs in and out of toes as tiny fish
    swim in the shallows

fishing fleet appears, all beach people stand, shade
    eyes . boats roll in on small surf waves, men
    jump ashore, self-conscious, busy with ropes,
    buckets, rods, reels and tackle . they winch
    boats to tractors, then carry the catch to
    the cutting block – a giant jarrah trunk that

seemingly grows out of the reef – there is
no time for beauty here : queen schnapper
swede black arsed cod pink salmon dhufish
giant red gropers lose their bright brilliant
seacolours so quickly : knives slice fillets out ...
first mate washes white meat in ocean waters
of the reef – yappy Harold slinks off with
the skins . audience stands about, stubbies in
hand, talking loud to be overheard : just like
a cooking demonstration – *you don't cut on the
rocks unless you cut bloody good* . fish flash fleshy
pinks and greens, bright red skins, bluey/yellow
scrambleline designs, scales *big as ashtrays*
. nullaguy eyes roll cold on the rocks, their
surprise swims in the sea

o

tonight
we eat fruit of the sea
as heads roll out
in the evening tide

beside her pillow
little Margie places
tiny seashells
found in giant fish guts

biggest treasure
on Upper Third Avenue

MELROS BEACH

Afternoon sun on Melros tints my skin as I walk
Among the dead the tide swept up to give us life.

Now sponges have shapes like clouds, now evoke
The same imagery: bones, breasts and lover's legs.

The forecast is for more of the same. You agree
Your sky and mine ramble freely, with some cloud.

Can we change? We wish and don't change. Again
We don't know. We try. I look out to sea.

Night crackles. Black sea lights up, all whales,
Dolphins and fish electrocuted. We play cards.

from *Pushing at Silence*

ELEGANCE

The fly has his own elegance
robed in wings so fine,
legs muscled like a spring.

He washes
at rest on the edge
of my page. My world
stops spinning as I
focus on this animal act –
no plumbing to mend,
car to fix or
mortgage in his world –
he flies off. I type
my envy, sitting
in a green tracksuit,
reading glasses on,
legs slack muscled,
ankles crossed above
outsize ugg boots.

He admires my elegance
as he shares my coffee
gone cold, just right.

POETRY HOUSEKEEPING

In this month's edition of
Poetry Housekeeping we tell
what to do with leftover

dactylics and why it's
a no-no to mix
objective correlatives

with Banjo balladry. Read
how to reply
 should a critic call you

'new wave'. Don't
be caught napping:
royal feminism may be

the next wave! Keep
that Tranter tan
with oodles and oodles

of Sydney studio neon –
Poetry Housekeeping tells how!
then slip between our covers

when Gwen Harwood meets
Komninos. Has she sold out?
Is he buying in?

It's all in
this month's edition of
Poetry Housekeeping,

under the counter
wherever culture
is sold.

WHALE'S EAR IN A COUNTRY MUSEUM

What does she hear now
in the inland museum

through the frozen light of
liquid sand, stones packed

tight, the crossed arms
of cultivated land, what

does she hear of her
once-body flowing

at one with the tide's
roaring silence in

coastal lanes of
instinct and song?

Who recognised her
to bury her here

in a sandy pocket of
civilisation's old coat?

My senses leap to
resuscitate her

with ceremony –
song, dance, tale.

We shuffle on
in our aimless day

to have afternoon tea
with the arts committee.

THE PIANOLESS QUARTET
for Alice

5.45pm I drive to pick-up
my daughter from Woolworths.
Hot evening, I park undercover,
browse at *Music Galore*. My
music's in the cheap bins now,
new CDs reviving Bird's bebop,
Billie's plaintive cry. I pick up
Mulligan's pianoless quartet.
In the Fifties Father sang schmaltz
while his friend, a Crosby fan
in cravat and velvet fog voice,
played *White Christmas* on
a three-note keyring harmonica.
We hid outside. Now Nat and Bing
are in the cheap bins with Duke,
Miles and Monk. I flick through,
standing in the mall like
a Russian doll, Father inside,
his father inside him. 6pm
her till rings off. We drive
through half deserted streets –
To break the silence I share
the 'pianoless quartet' story. She
shows me her new shoes.

MARY ANN AT KOOKYNIE CEMETERY

The Church of the Bleeding Heart
gave a damn to Mary Ann
who now lies estranged in death
from her Kookynie neighbours.
An out-of-town stone mason
cut 'In Loving Memory'.
I focus but don't shoot.
The bush crosses its mulga arms
above her clay bed. I stand by her,
shivering, wondering what
in her last days undid her as
art students pick at a quandong
whose roots suckled from Mary Ann
and raised her to sun and air.

1899.
Who she was has stopped here,
emptying of shadows and quarrels.
forty-four. No-one is too young.
I have a bad desire to dig her up
again, to ask the dumb questions
of any mortal still tied
to his goddamn days. I walk back to
the bus, camera strap around my neck,
seeing my shadows and quarrels
in her, holding off that
delicious piece of life
until last.

NONE SO RAW AS THIS OUR LAND

Many have been more exotic places, but this
you offer us, a taste of our land. The air
so crisp with chill we wear entire wardrobes
like hunters' furs – jeans over track pants,
footy socks, beanies, scarves. Mary's roo dog
does our hunting: an emu caught at the throat,
plucked and thrown whole on a cooking fire,
smoke full of singed feathers and flesh
stings our noses. We wrestle with tin-canned
standards in words the wind blows away. Huddled
round campfires morning and night, we go where
the sun breaks through as day unrolls. Breakaways,
mulga bush, a never-used dam a hundred years old,
this place of bleached bones and broken glass
queries our presence, unwashed, awkward on
its unpaved ways. Marrakesh, Katmandu – tales
of former hikes, but none so raw as this our land.
Whose land? Our week is up; we take away
film rolls, rusted horse shoes, ochre rocks.

NATURAL SFX
for Geoff Page

Standing at the edge of
the Western Desert,
minus two degrees Celsius,

I listen for
silence. Moon late,
campers asleep,

fires out, I hear
a distant road train
kicking up red dirt

like a country and western song
when all you want is
the white space between

church bells tolling.
Frogs listen too
between the lap-

slapping of
Niagara Dam's hundred-year-old
waters on

red rock shore. It's
as close as I'll ever hear to
hearing nothing,

like Basho atop
an old craggy mountain.
Charles Tomlinson writes

it rings true: for
silence / is an imagined
thing. Listen

ESSE EST PERCIPI
for Denis Cherry

I lie on the surgery table
staring up at the hanging
anatomical drawings of the forestry
around the skeletal frames
of man and woman, and trace
the muscle that pulls at
my leg from my lower back.
I'm in pain and now I know why.
Upfront I joke with my friend,
the doctor. He sees my eyebrows,
my laughing eyes, the leaping fish
in my mouth. You see, he says,
meaning I understand, then
loses me in medico lingo. I
wander, see him in two plays
on the same stage. To him
I am also a double bill: he sees
under my waves to my currents
and caves. Lap lap goes my blood,
following itself in blind obedience
like a bloodworm from river's edge.
Does he sense my fear? I see
he is curious, like a mechanic
with an out-of-tune engine.
Your timing's wrong, he could say
and it would be no surprise; I am
driven by analogies and abstract ideas.
I back away until I back into
somebody coming the other way,
a boy who couldn't cry at fourteen
and blamed his father for dying.

AUTOBIOGRAPHY

each block of wood
a head to chop

each plant
earth pushing up

the whistling wind
an open cloak

river rock crabs
drowned sailors' hands

every shadow
a sundial arm

SHARP-SMELLING MIST

I see us now on the cliffs
of the Swan River by
the slumbering suburb
where my brother and I fought,

running up slants of
sunlight, gripping rocks
and holding roots, then
sliding back twenty feet

on hands and knees
salted with rocksand,
blood running like
a river like memory.

I hear rock crabs
in jars under beds,
scuttling like pirates
on coral islands, caught

by boys who hired rowboats
with girls in springtime
from Smith's boatshed,
now Mead's Fish Gallery.

Today, fish swim
across screens like
jeering children behind
glass, and scuttling

in backflow from
earbuds on Walkmans –
Then floats to now
in sharp-smelling mist,

blowfish rotting on jetties,
rowboats driftwood to shore,
cars wrapped around trees,
friends torn like ragdolls,

then to now like a timetable
used to wrap gutted fish,
blood seeping through
onto salted hands.

MR HOBBY'S POPPIES

One poppy bends in the wind
precarious as
my memory of our driveway

bordered by poppies –
yellow, orange, white –
planted by Mr Hobby

knobbly old gardener who
spent one day a week
at our home.

Although we could afford
a dozen new sprinklers
he strapped and washered

old piping together
to create his own.
No better portrait

could have been
sculpted of the old
scrawny scarecrow

rusty brown and bent
torn cloth chokers
stained and wet.

They stuttered
and barely worked
all summer.

One poppy in the wind
rewinds me
forty years …

THE PERFUME FACTORY

The Ford *Customline* barrelled towards Long Point for our seaside holiday, with Mother shouting *Slow down, Adie!* over us six children fighting in the back. We had passed the War Memorial on the hill, the limestone walls of Fremantle Prison, and the corner where Mr Baker was the butcher ... We had left the suburbs behind.

    ... then Father would say, *Uh-ho, hold your noses, here it comes – Mr Rushton's Perfume Factory.* We would pinch our noses and hold our breaths like there was poison in the air. Curiosity would open our fingers and we'd squawk as the smell bit our nostrils. *Pewww!* and fall back into the upholstery in gleeful faints—*That pongs!* Together we'd delight in our family joke, Mr Rushton's Perfume Factory, bodiless skins drying on sunshine racks.

TESTAMENT

You alive, Jamie? What're your odds,
my school friend? Then you were
one of the younger boys. Now
a couple of years mean nothing.

Am I to write your Will and Testament?
Our verandah budgerigars still chatter
that you talked with so fluently,
a tongue of flight.

Your life's reward is peritonitis,
peripheral neuritis, wrecked liver
and voices off. You spend your days
talking crazy in city parks, hospitals,
doss houses and detox centres
saying you're too far gone ...

You have no mother. She
has changed her phone number, taken
her name from the directory.
Your brother has moved house.

You eat what you can get
and walk like a weather-beaten animal:
a dog, a horse, a man.

All winter you lived out
at railway stations
or crouched in the bushes
around the Dingo Flour Mills.

~

Pre-dawn light. Noises
outside our window where my wife and I
sleep. Scuffling animal noises, we wake
in fear. I open our door to find you
retching in our flowerbeds.
'Jamie, Jamie, where have you been?'
You fall into a chair, patchwork cushion
graciously placed. A bad smell
comes off your skin, that jacket,
ratty slacks, broken sneakers. No shirt.
'Where'd the jacket come from?'
'Last night some guy lent i
You look away. You had been dry
a year – social workers and therapists
had your name pencilled on their files.

'I don't want him here when the kids
wake up.' The kids walk out. They
have seen you like this
before, you don't frighten them.
I shudder and push you into our car.
I drive away from my family,
knowing this trouble, been there
myself, sitting next to a man …

~

That's when you nearly killed us,
trying to rip the radio out
when it wasn't on, hearing
race-calls as I drove down

Stirling Highway like an ambulance,
too fast, half awake, grabbing at you
as I drove up on the traffic island:
'Cut it out or you'll kill us both!'
Suddenly you settle back to tell me
about the race-caller, dead for years,
who is calling in your head. I drive
faster: 'I know a doctor,
he'll help, Jamie, he'll help.'

~

'Go away.' A gruff female voice.
'Can we see the doctor? My friend's sick.'
'I bet he is.' Disembodied voice, racked
with failure. 'He's out …' Doc opens
the door a crack. Some tired trick
of recognition makes him open it fully.
'James,' he says, flatly. The rooms are
shabbier than I remember, almost bare.
He reads my eyes. 'You been here before?'
'Yeah, in the old clinic days.'
'Government put us out of business,
we couldn't survive.' His sentence
dismisses years. 'Now, James.
still giving it a belting, I see,
you know what you're doing, I guess,
surprised you're still with us, do you
want to die?' All said in
a very tired rush. 'No and yes.' We nod.
'So what can I do? Tried ADA, hospitals?'
'Yeah. No go.' 'Hearing voices?' 'Race calls.'
A sour laugh. 'That'd be right.' He writes.

'I'll give you Hemies this time, James, but
don't come back. There is nothing I can do,
and I'm tired of all this trouble.'

~

Down the highway I pull into a pharmacy,
unwashed, unshaven, in raggedy jeans.
The shopgirl looks at me suspiciously
over jellybeans and sunscreens. 'Can I
help you?' She thinks I'm a junkie. 'Yeah,
could you fill this, please?' She takes
the scripts and locks heads with the chemist.
I try on sunglasses. He steps down. 'I'm afraid
we don't carry this stock.' Smug bastard.
'Do you know who does? My friend is
very sick.' He pauses, then –
'I'll try.' I try on wire frames,
casually. He returns with
a West Perth address. I leave
to find Jamie walking circles, talking
to everyone and no-one.

~

West Perth, we do our stop. After,
I buy Jamie a half bottle of brandy,

he downs it with pleasure, my nerves shot.

~

'Why'd you bring him back here?'
It's Saturday, the kids are home.
Our youngest asks, 'Do you drink?'
Jamie tries to bowl a ball in reply
but falls in the garden. We let him lie.
I phone the usual places. At
The Bridge I find a friendly ear,
says he'll call back if a client
doesn't show. We don't wait, we go.

'Looking after Number One,' he laughs.
'Even so, you're not home yet.'
Jamie takes the breathalyser test, I
fill in a form. We ruffle a bed
to show it's taken, punch a pillow.
Jamie shivers in a chair. I make coffee,
at home here, so lost that this is
the best I can do.

THE ROSARY BEADS

Sunday morning, I sit to
tie up my shoelaces
and see Christ on his Cross hanging
before me off the end of the bed.
Memories rise and I remain
bent over with one loop
in one hand, the other
in the other. What do I believe?
My wife wears these beads as
decoration. I've told her about
the priest's blessing, the way
we were taught to burn
all blessed items when they were no longer
wanted. Better than throwing Christ out
with the rubbish. Someone has
donated their rosary to a charity store
and placed generations of
counting the decades and my first beliefs
among dog-eared Reader's Digests,
foam wig stands and Bakelite mantle radios,
to be sold as glitter for an eye,
to be hung on the end of our bed
where last night we rolled and rose again.
He is such a small, white Christ
and his cross has buckled in the heat,
perhaps once hung in a taxi, or
left in a pocket through the hot cycle
of a Laundromat dryer. A simple thing
to be put away with other beliefs,
yet I reach out to cradle him in my hand.

LITTLE WHITE PILLS

The little white pills
have their names
chiselled in them
like hieroglyphs.

Beside them on
the draining board
lies a watermelon seed,
waiting to surprise the earth.

I swallow the pills
and hold the seed:
if I could change my life
I would, I would.

WALKING TO THE MEETING

Walking to the meeting,
sixteen years sober,
I watch my weight.

The hospital street is
quiet as a night ward.
Sandwiched between

Emergency and Morgue
this 12 Step meeting
is as comfortable as

an old tracksuit. I've
forgotten how it feels
to be drunk, to

have the shakes
on a Sunday morning.
It takes a newcomer to

shake me up again.
His eyes dart from
ceiling to floor

and don't see a thing.
He shakes, he sweats,
he thinks we're all

watching him. He's
right. He is keeping
us sober if only

he knew it. I talk,
I remember yesterday
and tell my story:

the ism in youth,
alcohol in teenage years,
self-disgust in adulthood ...

but I am going
too far, addicted
to my story, the drama

loved more than
drink. I quickly finish
on a local cliché:

'This is my recovery
room.' I sit and smile
at the newcomer

but he is staring
at my shoes. And
I remember that, too.

THE KID'S LAST FIGHT

Bouncing off canvas,
fighting fire, smoke
and bureaucracy

has drawn gentle Ben
to the surface
through all his days

of fireman and tent boxer.
Every-boy's-dream sits
in a neutral corner,

dubious legs crossed –
a legacy of chasing
the masculine,

to be a bloke
in this
jockstrap city.

Today he closes
his frayed
'Kid Wild' gown

around
wrinkled genitals,
a lifetime of girls

in his pulse, the call
'Go, Kid, go!'
down sawdust aisles.

Even now they bathe
his knuckles
in the Extended Care Ward.

Between rounds
he grips their hands:
'All I ask's a slow count –

'Ya with me?
Eh? eh?
eh?'

THE PRESESSION

You're leaving your run
a bit late, he said,
looking at my birthdate

on the form. These
formulated questions
presume so much

that life is neat,
that events come in
tidy packages like

numbers on a clock
the way a bank statement
tells you everything

and nothing about
your money, how
you spent your life

working for enough
to eat and sleep
out of the rain,

how you came to
this, a young man
secure at his desk

handing you more forms,
telling you about
how late it is.

From *Whispering Gallery*

RAINY DAYS

No wipers so I curse the rain and drive like a blind shepherd lost in his flock. Out of my car and into her house, the rain follows me, a stowaway in my jeans, jumper, socks and sneakers. Such a squall the fire sizzles with rain driven down the chimney by tangential winds. Her cat growls as I take his chair before the fire.

She offers me shelter from the storm, dries my hair and whispers in my ear, *Wanna fool around?* Then turns down her bed to accept me like a dolphin in the womb of the sea. The Earth's pulse beats in the ocean, and rain rises to fall again.

A CEREMONY OF SORTS

The marriage took a cathedral, three vintage Rolls Royces, four groomsmen and four bridesmaids and one flowergirl to happen. Fifty and more friends drank until they were falling over and goosing the waitresses. The next morning we made the cover of *The Sunday Times*.

Today I sit with six sheets of official papers and read instructions from the Do-It-Yourself Divorce Kit. It's too early to light the fire and I shiver. Only the cat lives with me now. I fill out the forms slowly, stumbling over dates, forgetting places. I go to the kettle and cup my hands in its steam – a ceremony of sorts, as much as this day brings.

THE OLD TAMBOURINE

Job interview over I change
into old jeans, a T-shirt that says
"Happy Dad's Day" in my daughter's
young hand, and pull on gloves I have
borrowed from my eldest son. A bin
from Pete's Gold Bins waits out the front
of Number 3, two cubic metres to hold
ten years detritus at this address. We
have told the children, and now
we're trying to accept the fact ourselves.
I walk to our back corner. Between shed
and fence lies a fetid mess of limbs,
broken cement slabs, old pots and   I
start at the top. An hour and I'm
dripping. I have excavated through
tree limbs and broken garden pots to
pockets of worm-holed business ledgers,
shattered hand mirrors, and bright
plastic toys from childhoods now closed.
My hand frees an old tambourine,
skin gone, cymbals rusted and wood stained with the sap of severed limbs. I slap it against my elbow, and it crumbles. Sweat stings my neck where I shaved this morning as I throw the pieces into the bin. A half-burnt train. Red lego. A stuffed sky-blue unicorn, misshapen now like a dead mouse. Tonight I'll retire early, tired, avoiding talk. We grow back our skins, every seven years we reupholster. Pete's Gold Bin is overflowing, so I step in in my old gardening boots to stomp, to jump up and down, to compress the rubbish into its fit space.

'THE SIMPLE TRUTH' MEDITATION
The Simple Truth is a poem by Philip Levine

*Some things
you know all your life. They are so simple and true
they must be said without the elegance of rhyme,
they must be laid on the table beside the saltshaker,
the glass of water, the absence of light gathering
in the shadow of picture frames, they must be
naked and alone, they must stand for themselves.
Some things you know
must be said with diligence; they must be turned
hand over hand at the table when all else
has retired to the fireside. Other things
you know need nurturing like bulbs; they will
return in their own season, all your life.
Prayers of childhood, sounds of first love,
Balinese breakfasts.
Some things you know,
others escape you. We are made of such
things, a ragbag of faith and deeds. it is obvious,
it stays in the back of your throat like a truth
you never uttered because the time was always*
wrong, it stays there for the rest of your life, unspoken, a love undisclosed, her smile at her husband's funeral re-screened twelve times a day for nourishment, for nourishing the life left in you all your life, the undeclared beat in your pulse. You'll go to your grave silent with the things you know, like any ethical spy, and in a possible after life there will be new perspectives. They say the dead sit up in crematoria, naked, alight, alone, and out of their mouths comes the smoke of their perceptions, like exhalations on a cold morning in corridors of light.

MANDALA WOK

The washing up water bubbles
into a fine froth, doing its job as

I wash the wok from last night,
soaking off the burnt noodles.

The swirl of water rests
as I daydream out the window

till I look down and there
lies perfect yin yang

white suds, black wok,
mandala for Monday.

REGIONAL AEOLIAN

>Sometimes you must squint to see
things right, as through a glass darkly
the joy beyond. Other times nature's
lines are straight, a four-four beat
between bars. If within me balance
drew nigh ... There's a composer in
this town who bought a stretch of
deserted powerlines down by Esperance
to record Aeolian music, ethereal as
wind washed by waves, the chill off
icebergs, a span of albatross wings,
the drumming of a drowned choirboy's
bones. I asked, *Do you tune them?*
He turned sharply, then softened at
my naiveté: *I am sometimes tempted,*
he said – gently, in confidence, Aeolian
in tone – *tempted. Often,* I said, *I am too.
And were you an altar boy? There is
something Gregorian about the way
the ocean sings to the land.*

In the early Sixties, we leapt out of a two-tone Holden under a sky intensely blue, air rippling off the earth, we came upon waves of white sand rolling to the ocean's edge. Old Eucla town had moved inland, their dead left buried behind. Out into the Southern Ocean, a jetty failed towards the horizon. Whooping like boys, we ran to its first extant timbers and clambered its limbs, limbs like slippery railway sleepers, prickly with molluscs. Cautiously we picked our way through sheets of sky and ocean, then ran, leaping missing planks, until twenty metres out we dived into the air.

THE GOD BOTTLE

> Each day is a square off the calendar,
> like not knowing when to stop
> unwrapping a papier mâché sculpture
> of yourself. 'I have measured out my life
> in coffee spoons' was the original but
> you can substitute what is relevant
> for you. Maybe its relevance is
> a banister to hold. Coffee spoons are
> a collectible now, under Cutlery,
> sub-section Teaspoons to place them
> in their tradition. Next it will be
> Prozac containers – each church has
> its faithful. The markings set each item
> apart – any text, colour, condition
> and date of manufacture – each
> collectable's bio-data. Archaeologists
> dig up bones and the poet picks over
> them, doodling in calendar squares.
> Soon he has a little model of
> his days and ways.

'I knew a guy once who had a God bottle. I'm serious – he had a clear glass two litre flagon, and he called it his God bottle. Every time he didn't know what to do about something in life – simply whether to or not to do something, maybe a moral question, or how to make amends – he would write it down on a piece of paper and shove it in this bottle. He passed his will and his life over to the care of God (as he understood him) and mailed his concerns in his God bottle. This way he was never paralysed by indecision or self-doubt. It worked for him.'

from *Undercover of Lightness*

AS WE ARE

Before he drives off, my friend asks,
Do you remember desperate times?

All day, so much speech, so little
meaning, parallelisms on rhetorical
bars. 'I am adjustable,' say the shorts'
monologic care tag. As we are.
Adamson to Creeley, *These days
we're just words away from death.*

Here I play my lexicon kit, constructing,
melodic, breath and tongue whistling
above the rattle-tattle of my bones.

GOING HOME

As I exit, I walk by my books in the uni
library. There is a shorter way but I
choose to hear my old words whispering
off the shelf *in the swarm of human
speech*, as Duncan said. On my way home,
in the safe bubble of my Japanese car,
I take the tunnel and in the humming
dark inexplicably think of
my White Russian friend naked on
his chopper, whooping loudly in his flight
across the desert, ejaculating in ecstasy
on his fuel tank. Those were the days,
my friend. Now, my tunnel breaks
into sunlight. The poet I visited today said,
Even the poems are chatty now, and he
was right: at the red traffic light
lines come to mind and I hurry to
write them down. The lights change
and my pen dries out. Diesel fumes invade
my thoughts so I turn the volume
up on ABC Jazz to drown out my
annoyance. That motel has been there
for decades. I remember the one-eyed
mother, with her baby in a cot, offering
me her love, or something masquerading
as that, in dusky afternoon light, a room
rented after fleeing her husband, the sound
of peak hour traffic slowing as it banked
for the suburbs. I'm off in a dream world
when the car behind me toots, and I'm
on the road again. Her name has gone

but her eye patch remains and the baby's
sweet snuffling. I change to a pop music
station. Get out of your own head, I
advise myself. It's not safe there, the
past is corrosive. At home I park
and leave the bubble of car and poem
with its own centrifugal force.

SHOP LOCALLY

'Keith the Butcher is better suited
to conduct my funeral than
Father Fahey,' Frank said in
the shopping centre café, coffee tasting
like burnt tar, muffin crumbling
on his off-white face.
Mock-stained-glass windows framed
consumers relieving aching backs
and knotted veins. 'None of that God stuff
when they send me off, mate.
Dead's dead.' I forewent
a second cup, mentally ticked
off my list, threaded fingers through
handles of Coles supermarket bags,
and stood to go. 'See ya, mate.'
'Not if I see you first.'

In the car park, shopping propped
against the back bumper, I clicked
'unlock', threw open the boot,
and paused, considering the metaphors
of everyday, cryptic tropes of our living tongue
wriggling in the minds of
late capitalist man. 'Hot enough for you?'
asked the woman with
The Goddess Dances on her rear window.

SHOPPING CENTRE GENIUS
"the nothingness of human matters" - de Man quoting Rousseau

    How many suburban shopping centres
    have I walked, only to see you
    in the eyes of the man
    who wanders rootless by himself,
    torn summer t-shirt and hooded
    winter jacket. He isn't you

    yet I see you in his faulty
    step forward, hear you in his
    every jumbled phrase
    in a patois of too many pills
    and sleepless nights. Bored,

    security guards nickname him
    Socrates or The Professor, then offer him
    the door, bowing, mock courteous
    in their security.

    They let you out yet locked you in,
    didn't they. Where once you debated
    the de Man question, now your day begins
    in a chemical blur through shrubbery
    sous rature in manicured gardens.

HAVE A NICE DAY

Driving to the shopping centre,
Bukowski rambling in my ear,
I'm glad to be sober
and anonymous. When I was
young, all hormones and energy,
my poetic was all about
getting laid. Today I step
from my Toyota, head full
of Buk, and grab a trolley, swearing
at its bent wheels. That'll help,
my sober brain puts in, sarcastic
as ever. I push and the old desire
to be listened to comes back
and I'm impatient at each counter,
waiting for this, waiting for that.
They've got machines now,
not people. Just key in
your late mother's hat size
and, *voila*, the money is out
of your account and into theirs,
Messrs Coles and Woolies. Warmly
I remember the décolletage of
Sandy with the metal in her nose,
tongue and ears. Where is she today?
At the scrap metal yard?
This machine doesn't rock my world.
It doesn't have Sandy's knowing smile,
asking sweetly through banded teeth,
Any fly bys? It's a drive-by, fly by,
bye-bye whirled. Who'll enjoy
fly bys on my funeral plan?

Buk's buggered my mood, but he's
dead and I'm still here, so
who's to complain. The machine
says, *Have a nice day* with
a metallic twang and I
kick the trolley straight again.

SNAP DRAGONS

snap dragons
swaying in
a childhood garden

continue to
snap here
in my old mind

APOLOGIA

The poem I wrote for her was for me – all ego –
that's how I see it now: a masquerade party,
with me posing and knowing, confident confidant.

The imagery was measured, cut
from day's marble of sun and shade;
and I spoke of her *bejeaned arse* like a boy

saying things to shock his mother, cheeky,
not downright rude. Cheeky too
the *curve of breast* – somehow the road

carried my load, red motorbike's roar
my mating call to her. It is so
predictable now, looking back …

I cut away the glissando and the Boy's Own
Symbolism, I cut out the pose and the poise;
I cut a page down to a quatrain. Will she

see me now? I'm in plain view, ego
lightened by the light of years, a boy
leaning on his bike outside her house.

FACTORY LIFE

At Arctic Coldstores, we called him Bill,
the Box-biting Bastard of Ballarat.
The Dutch foreman was Andy –
he'd wave his fists and say, 'I'm 'andy
with these too!' We laughed
coz he was the foreman, but he had
more moods than a chameleon.

My role: to release
ammonia to the freezer rooms.
I escaped to the attic up a steel ladder –
cold at night, too hot at midday.
Down there they wore big black ape suits
to bear the cold, while above them
I sweated like a boy
on his first promise. I'd turn
the wheels sticking up from an inlet pipe
with great difficulty – ammonia
had frozen it to the pipe.
The far one was a bastard
it needed a metal bar wedged
in its wheel to get loose. I chanted,
fuckin' bastard, stupid cunt of a thing,
trying to be one of the boys.

Why wasn't I happy to be a human being?

'Hey, you finished up there, you useless bastard?'

THE OPTHALMIC PROSTHETIST

Back then
I shared an office with
an ophthalmic prosthetist.

Rows of eyes,
dusted with a fine white powder,
stared everywhere.

He himself had
a masterpiece in one socket,
an eye for a dollar in the other.

With his checked sports jacket,
knife edge pleated slacks
and clouds of after shave,

he was the original
slick dick – his favourite
house, the Happy Haven.

What the whores thought of him
I have only his bragging to tell …

Sometimes, as a laugh,
he would wear a blue eye
and wink with his hazel one.

'for days I have watched in wonder'

for days I have watched in wonder
                         the muscular bodies of
                 ants as they have climbed
the stony path to the
                 firebreak at the bottom of this block
                         in the greatest heat of day –
               well over 40 degrees Celsius –
walking furiously
                               frenetically
between rocks over sticks between leaves
                never
                      seeming to
catch breath
                   never stopping   never resting
unless   just now
                  at the salty pool of my
             sweat droplet
                       crashing to earth
on their set path

ON THE THIRD DAY

In the first days of winter
mushroom pop-ups like
childhood toys litter
the pristine park

White domes with no
'use by' on them, no bar-codes
for value judgement. In the wetness
and warmth they grow as dogs
trot by with their gossiping owners.

A tiny Vietnamese lady, in
a brilliant yellow anorak, crosses
the street, bucket and trowel in hand.
I watch. She knows
the ways of survival,
she harvests every dome.

Passing schoolchildren point
and laugh, but she hears kookaburras
high in the gums. Winter's false start
brings her back for three mornings. I wait
and harvest her across busy lanes of traffic.

ON CHAPMAN HILL
for Pablo and Jenny

Let's walk to get the city out
of our bones. I'll show you red gums,
xanthorrhea with spears, flame-tailed
black cockatoos – no strangers here
unless you hear the protea's accent
on the evening breeze.

See, kangaroos' paws break
the tractor tread marks, while
off that stony corner a body rusts,
wings and bonnets, flat trays
and drive shafts, welded
wildly by the elements.

Tonight, you'll hear boobooks
stretch silence horizon to horizon
in bright moonlight. It sends
Pancho into a barking frenzy,
shouting down the ghost in the trees –
attack his best line of defence.

Sure as day follows night, there's
growth in decay. This land, once
Noongar, is now plotted and pieced. By
the water tank, old Buddha stands silent,
eyes hooded among raindrops sparkling
on gum leaves in sudden sunlight.

DETAILS

The house whispers
its discontent and keeps me up
with its incessant whining.
The trick would be to turn off,
like the filament in the bedside lamp
when I press the plastic button
beneath the shade. The physics
of the real world, not the metaphoric,
are life without you: the dozen
details of each event – bringing in
The West Australian, shaking it free
of dewdrops, watering your plants,
removing my wet sandals. Details.
Like the atmospheric control light
I've never noticed in
the refrigerator before. Beep,
it complains. Beep. Beep. Details
like that. I can tell you now
you're so far away how many
steps lead from the front door to
the letterbox. The house rises before me
and clears each room of any life
that might be there to join me
as I rise from my chair, walk out, say
'Hello?', return and read
your itinerary again.

DOROTHY DOROTHY DOROTHY
i.m. Dorothy Hewett

Merv leaves the Blue Mountains
and returns, mumbling behind the wheel
of a hearse, *This hearse is
a raised finger at Death.*

currawongs call shadows to light

Merv passes lorries on the hill
but Dot's the navigator still

As they stop at each pit-stop
she falls in love with the waiter
who sings & tells dark-eyed lies

Merv's tinkering with the motor
adding a little oil
more air to a back tyre

last rays of day long
Dorothy addresses Death:
*'We see what you've been doing
taking more than your fair share
we're on to you ...*

*You come knocking like
JWs. Tell those who believe
your poppycock. Try next door –
they're an unhappy bunch.'*

WRITING ON A BROWN BAG IN FREO
i.m. John Forbes

I write on a brown paper bag,
The Collected Poems of John Forbes inside.

    See, over there,
  a young man in everything black
    waves his guitar, present tense,
at the traffic in Freo's High Street.
    He crosses to *New Edition*. Perhaps
I bought the book he wanted
  to spend his busking money on.

How our days are *The Collected*,
our faces in the street, poems
pinned to each page
reverently. I want to put
coffee rings on each one, a little
weed here and there, sprinkle
a proprietary pharmaceutical line
over all …

  Our busker doesn't have
    a guitar case, his strings open
to the weather, face grimacing at
    the diesel exhaust of buses before
a night playing in human exhaust.

In our lives' raggedy paths we had
furniture removal in common –
mattresses, beds, wardrobes,
jarrah drawers, even old Frigidaires
with their round shoulders and weird handle,
too heavy for the wages.
Already the myths need regassing.

So now I write on a brown paper bag,
    John Forbes inside. I shake him
like a rattle: echoes spill, click-clack rhythms
    of the heart. I take *The Collected* out, put
the bag to my lips, fill it with air
    and burst it on my knee.

The limits of my language are the limits of my world. WITTGENSTEIN
i.m. Tony Statkus

As bit players, the limits
of everyday activity
are the limits of our lives. You are
half out the door, going
who knows where. Perhaps you can
tell us when we meet again.
We don't expect cards or letters,
emails or texts, and only our
limited senses would ask for
photos of the other side.

Did you leave your watch behind?
I picture Sue running
after you, shouting, 'You forgot
your watch, you forgot your watch.'
Time is only for us now,
empty arms of the clock
hold us back from joining you.
When you were sick
and tired of it all, you left. I can
understand that. Mind the step,
wipe your feet. I expect we will follow you
in time. They chisel years
on tombstones, don't they, yet facts
are putty in historians' hands after deeds
are done. It's a variety show, all this song and dance.
Total it up: More love than hate,
more laughter than tears. Do you need
a torch? Or is that light at the end of the tunnel
light enough? Perhaps you can send us
a clue or two, telling us what happens next?
Eh? Tell me that.

BAD WEATHER
i.m. Dorothy Porter (1954-2008)

Dear Dorothy – grey clouds are
apt today here in Summertime.
Your body is still above ground.
To end novels is one thing: planned,
edited. Not life. My wife is
inside the hospital now where
they explore her breasts.
Brings me back to reality, if I
ever left it. Light rain falls. I lean
on a railing and watch the river ripple.
In the halls of academe and in
the literary press, they'll speak
of your writing as 'her work', complete,
reading meaning into its inconclusiveness.
Friends will file away
your ironic smile with your titles.
Rain falls heavier now, hailstones
ping off cars below. My mind shrugs:
questions of mortality are stale. If
we could rewrite your final days,
we would, we would.

PADDLER
for Andrew Taylor

memories mark time
peppered with days and nights
loves, house and children
a train ticket, a photo in Europe

peppered with days and nights
dawn's long shadow –
a train ticket, a photo in Europe
tail feathers of a kite

dawn's long shadow
ripples over rocks –
tail feathers of a kite,
a mountain stream

ripples over rocks,
yesterday's rain runs
a mountain stream
to the river, to the coast;

yesterday's rain runs
down leaves, off dry sands
to the river, to the coast.
rafts of sunlight flash

down leaves, off dry sands
to a paddler in midstream.
rafts of sunlight flash,
drop from the blade

of a paddler in midstream –
echoes of great rivers
drop from blade,
generation upon generation

echoes of great rivers,
loves, houses and children,
generation upon generation,
memories mark time

WASHING
at Tom Collins House

Today you won't see one
but back in the Sixties
the historic house I lived in had
a timber and wire clothesline,
propped up in mid string
by the long sapling of a eucalypt tree
which forked at the top and held up
the sagging line. Urban Aborigines,
out of work and down on their lunch,
walked door to door selling these props,
cut down on bush walks out of town.
With over six metres of sheets and nappies
flapping in an easterly off the desert, strong wires
hung loose between two crucifixes
with movable arms. On the night of a full moon
a small feathered woman would arrive
and sit on top of the post near
the gnarled and knotted mulberry tree,
her wisdom silent in her,
two deep eyes focused on me
as I wrote by moonlight,
sitting on the back steps,
pad resting on sunburnt knees.

WASHING DAY

I hang my washing out in a light drizzle.
Neighbours on their way to cars, say, *Good morning*.
I reply, *Good morning*.

Should I explain? *You see, what happens is ...*

No. It is a subject for them to talk about on the way to the air-conditioned cinema in their air-conditioned car. The weather is always outside. They have dryers. Even their hair needs dryers.

I go inside.

There is a puddle where my washing dripped on the linoleum. On my boots I bring garden leaves out of the rain where shirts happily flap their arms in a light breeze.

A DAY IN THE LIFE

My chest clenches
and I fumble in my pocket
for the Nitrolingual spray.

I'm walking
my damaged heart and dog
through tall gums.

You can watch so much
television, you can nap
just so many hours

then you itch
to do things, simple things
like stretch your legs

and walk.
I stand under a tree
to catch its breath.

A Nitrolingual mist
is working its way
through dank slums

to open the way ahead.
Zimmy sits at my feet, tongue
hanging like

a flag at half mast.
'Come on,' I say,
'let's go.'

DIARY: ROYAL PERTH HOSPITAL

I am Bed 6GC
beside the helipad.

Identity band on
they won't lose me
I'll know who I am.

There's a ghost of myself
on this bed's TV –
star of my memories.

My daughter brings
Rolling Stone, National Geographic,
this page for
these thoughts.

My right leg, groin and chest
are shaved – skin white

I shower
put stockings on

Helicopter lands
a well-wrapped
lump of humanity –
man, woman or child –
is drawn from its belly.

Pilot has a cup of tea.

o

5.30am operation day
Nurse Uwe wakes me.

I'm in a hospital gown,
arse hanging out,
bow tied behind my head.
I wait for pre-med. I'm not nervous
yet. Six months since
my heart's silent ambush.

o

Christ and his two thieves
left their crosses
at the cathedral next door:

weathered concrete,
not a splinter on them.

'It's just a story,' the chaplain says.
'You should know that, Andrew.'

I grew up with Christ's thorns
tattooed on my brain.

When Veronica wipes away my wounds,
all pain will join the clouds
gathering for this day.

o

When the orderly collects me
he is tall, an urbane African.

We speak of cross-
rhythms and syncopation.

He humours
my nervous prattle

as he pushes my bed
down corridors
into lifts to theatre.

o

The operating team
wear theatre costumes
but the spotlight is on me.

My Greek chorus
leans in leans out,

the room waves,
fades to
black.

o

Day Two

Brittle bones, rechanneled
blood and flawed heart,
I am drained of much
and live in echoes.

My faded book
whispers
of a bleak end.

o

Day Three

In ICU
logic is off its chain:

I am reduced to tears
as machines measure
ebb and flow of
days, nights worse
as choppers drop
squads of para-
noia troops—terrorists
attack through tubes
into the interior night
shadows of my brain,
a mind field. I am
reduced to fears.

US fast food outlet streets blaze
with orange and red strip neon lighting
flaring like over-exposed video images blazing
into tropical wet fields of Vietnamese farmers
and smoky Chinese street vendors

chopper mounted machinegun's manic rat-
a-tat-tat rips through
a happy jingle …

nightmare montage

o

Ward 6G

Late night, I watch
the 2010 Wimbledon Men's Final
Day Four after CABG surgery.
6 to 5 second set,
Nadal has control.

A woman in
the crowd has
my mother's hat on
last worn when
Rod Laver won the Cup.
Nadal and I aren't finished yet—
athleticism and technique will
see us through – *taking the pace off*
his backhand has given him the edge.
Ace. Nice mixture.
The runner-up: Tomas Berdych!
Audience applauds wildly.
Obese Bed K2 farts robustly,
Bed K4 snores to wake the dead.

It hurts to laugh
so I share silently
with my mother.

Now, late Night 4, I hug
an outsize scapula to my chest
containing ECG leads
and some connection to
childhood beliefs.

o

Day Five

Dawn
I walk the Ward.

I'm 'me' again
a paranoid wreck in

the high office of
the individual.

Don't tell them anything.
(imagine telling them that …)

I keep my eye on the Exit sign.

HOME FROM HOSPITAL

5am
that silent
time before dawn .

A kookaburra sings solo outside our courtyard.

On the windowsill
my old comb lies,
clogged with dog's hair.

Time is a measurement of change.

More kookaburras sing now,
like all the canned
laughter of TV's sit coms
played out of control.

I sit at the kitchen table
*(I have measured my life
in kitchen tables)*
attempting to write
a punch line before
the penultimate break.

UNFOLD
after Charles Bernstein

I love my love
I hate my hate
I feel my right
to write my right
just as the sky
feels right as night
breaks into day –
that is to say
I love my may
apply my choice
while I can voice
my love my hate
my right to write

UPSIDE-DOWN SONNET

'I'll give you to the next passing Chinaman',
my mother would say.
It was the Fifties and such things were said
without malice
for there were few passing Chinamen
in our home town.

Fifty six years later I am
an Australian man passing
and Chinese kids look up at me
without prejudice – a living
breathing specimen
of Western decadence,
The Coca-Cola culture come
flying over their wall.

BIKE MECHANICS

Flying Pigeon,
Forever Gold …
Racehorses? No –
bicycles in China,
made of low quality
Chinese steel so
soon they'll rust
but scoot through
the frenetic traffic
well enough.
There's one called
Alice, another *Sally.*

By the roadside
bike mechanics
work, squatting
among ballbearings,
broken spokes,
bent forks and
punctured tubes.
It reminds me
of my youth
as they check the valve
in a basin of water
and rasp the tube's
surface to patch it.
We had a clamp and
some kind of burning system
on our back veranda.
Here they work
on the ragged stone pavement,

among spilt noodles
and cigarette butts.
One old spark plug
lies on the pavement,
and a young boy,
opportunist at five,
picks it up and scurries away.
Maybe Dad will be pleased.

Here on the corner
where we walk
skipping puddles
and rotting refuse
a three-wheeler
with metal flat-bed on the back
is turned upside down.
They operate on its axle,
sticking things together again.
It's Humpty Dumpty
Engineering, and he's ready to go
in ten minutes or so –
but just now
he sells melons to
passers-by.
If it's daylight
it's business hours
for the poor melon sellers
of Linfen.

LINFEN MORNING

6.30am. The overture to day in Linfen is played with household hammers on commercial building projects. Cicadas sing gently in madrigal phrases. The irregular rhythm of the hammers gradually joins the first honking vehicles of morning, various toots on a full range of flutes. The street vendors put out their vegetables and fruits and squat beside. A few have weighing machines for basic conversion of goods to cash. There seems no hurry here, no anger, no overt competition, no conflict between workers and bosses. The town grows daily, and the shops change hands overnight. One man is gone from the streetscape. He wrote an anti-government message in his shop window and was not there the next day. A new shop has opened there now, selling fashion for young ladies.

By 8am the town is a bustle, going about its business. A pale grey smog hangs in the air which a light morning breeze seems incapable of shifting. Three mature citizens sweep away the remnants of last night's fireworks with bush-brush brooms.

> *at night, fireworks.*
> *at dawn, torn red paper shells*
> *dye the gutters pink.*

MORE RAIN TODAY
Late Summer, Linfen

More rain today than fell last year. Pollution
coats the buildings as rain falls perpendicular.
Linfen's drainage system overflows
and baby-faced police huddle in muddy vans
while the townsfolk welcome the wash:
a little soap in the alleys' armpits,
sunny deodorant with dawn perhaps.
Inside, street vendors huddle, stretching
yesterday's Yuans like old inner tubes.
The gatekeeper pulls a grey sheet over
his knobbly knees on his roadside cot.
Beyond Linfen city, farmers wave as
roads run with mud and crops drink deep.
Tomorrow shines like sunflowers in their eyes.

'Teaching now'

Teaching now
rows of blank faces
I can't read
staring at me
who they can't read.

Chalk dust in my throat
coaldust in my eyes
hot chillies in my mouth
market lanes full of
stick brooms and steaming vats
and fish that jump
from their troughs ...
Every step a surprise,
each sense assaulted.

I teach them to say *G'Day* –
something Australian
to combat the US influence.
Here we are in China
Bamboo Curtain down
but still ghostly felt.

Girls give themselves
English names of
abstract ambition –
Harmony, Enjoy,
even my favourite –
Sugarfree ☺

MANHOLE COVERS

'The beauty of manhole covers — what of that?
Like medals struck by a great savage khan,
Like Mayan calendar stones, unliftable, indecipherable,'
Karl Shapiro, *Manhole Covers* **(1968)**

'Bitten at the edges', Shapiro said, ex-
act, like here in this coalmining town,
Shanxi Normal University campus to be
exact, where we have learnt to shallow breathe
over manholes in the broad pathways
where god-knows-what passes underground
and perfumes the sulphuric air as
slim ladies in stylish spangled jeans go
riding by, two to a bike, one pedalling, one
balancing lightly on the carrier, like
corps de ballet ballerinas at a rubbish tip.
Those are particles in the air that offend
rising from exotic embossed shields
of ancient khan warriors, the ex-
acts of history nothing to
the attack on us
today.

EPISTLE TO ANDREW TAYLOR

Once upon a time I taught Beckett (some
wit said he needed teaching …) and now
I teach Oral English to students in China
on a Wednesday morning. I do it
for the money – a little extra
to buy poetry and jazz. Any teacher
of an oral language in any tongue
is playwright, producer, performer
and critic, a multi-headed beast with
his audience at heart. Sixty plus
Chinese faces look at me as exotica:
an unusual fish in a goldfish bowl,
passing by each week as it comes
around, pinkish-white, blowing bubbles
and feeding off their attention. My jokes
sink like lead weights. I cast about
for cultural bait to haul them in, but
the school is in one stream and I'm
from another, the tidal force as wild as
the traffic outside where the double-line
is just another line to cross. Adrenalin
helps the act, fear of
the audience is grist for the mill,
but I am 60 plus myself – each face
is a year on my playschool clock. I'm
of a different psyche and miss ocean
breezes, the sunshine as I walk outside
to retrieve the morning paper from
rose bush or eucalypt (so English, so
Australian). You write of
fine weather and bike rides on

paths and roads where sanity rules.
In this town alone there are
a million bikes, and donkeys and
bad-ass taxi drivers, trucks and vans.
To walk is an adventure, the pathways
reefs of debris and dangerous vehicles.
At 60 plus, their faces line mine,
the rush and intersection of language
like crazed cyclists with
bent wheels and nervous bells.

THE CLEAN AIR ACT OF 1956

> *The sunshine of the Land*
> *Of Sunshine is a gray mist now, the atmosphere*
> *Of some factory planet: when you stand and look*
> *You see a block or two, and your eyes water ...*
>   *Thinking of the Lost World* by **Randall Jarrell** (1965)

I dust off books from Shanxi Uni library –
the English books, that is. They are
donations from this or that organisation,
The Asia Foundation, Shanghai University,
or a library somewhere more salubrious
in the fabled West. Randall Jarrell
sits in a winding sheet of clean pages in
The Norton Anthology of Modern Poetry,
Second Edition. Chill Linfen air was
sulphurous this morning, and (add
a thick mist) walking to class was
dangerous. The bus between
campuses had its foghorn on.
Shanxi students studying for a *better* life
should rebel against the mine owners
for a *longer* life. I teach
English history: '*In response to*
   the Great London Smog *of*
December 1952, the Government intro-
duced its first Clean Air Act in 1956.'
London's death rate dropped. If I
know it, they know it, the bosses, as
their silver fins glide between weary donkeys
in the ancient streets of Linfin.

SNOW IN LINFEN

Pine trees bend with snow.

In their essays, Chinese students write 'dialectically' and 'imperialistic', words I haven't seen in a while. Japanese teacher Yoko asks, 'Do your students ask personal questions?' Each culture is different, but ironing jeans, in London, New York, Paris, Rome or Linfen, is a bourgeois sentiment.

They haven't weeded that roof in decades. Tree has no leaves but leaf-sized birds on every bough. It's not every day you can see your hand in front of your face. Shoebrush to brush away the dust, loses its bristles on first use. Toothbrush too.

This is life in China: fun and drama, upsets and pleasures. I quote Du Fu in English. 'You read Du Fu? In English? You don't read Du Fu.' In the seat of Chinese civilisation, vines cover a rusted fighter plane.

Yoko points at the word 'cormorants'. I answer, 'It is a bird that sits on pylons and rocks and dries its wings like this.' Idiogrammatic.

Student writes, 'Chinese is hieroglyphs, English is typing.' All writing is polis.

Linfen snow: white in the kindergarten, black on the roads.

TAIBAI MOUNTAIN POEM
for Jeanette

I saw a shining moon last night
through leafy poplars and pines
on Taibai Mountain
and thought of you awake
amid the lowing of Brahman bulls.

I thought of Li Bai
spilling ink down the mountain
leaving black stains
and wondered whose Dreaming
spilt red on The Kimberley?

LINFEN TAXI RIDE

Today is Monday so I rose early and went out to second campus by the uni bus at 7.20am. I taught freshmen Oral English until 10am and then caught a taxi back home. It is not expensive to catch a taxi here, but it is often exciting, sometimes dangerous. Today's driver was an anachronism in physical appearance. He looked exactly like a cartoon version of a 1950s/ early 1960s American hipster: about 30 years old, in a wide-lapelled, double breasted jacket with a dark shirt underneath, 'cool' sunglasses, a prickly black goatee beard with matching moustache, and a crazy haircut not unlike an old flat-top Kramer cut from those decades. When I sat down, he said 'Hell oh', gunned the tincan taxi out into the traffic, then grinned and said, all as one phrase, 'Hell oh satta down pleeze'. I liked his way of driving, fearless, fast and lyrical. He drove like I imagine Dean Moriarty of *On the Road* fame would have driven – or maybe the real man behind the wheel of Keroauc's novel, Neal Cassidy. My driver knew where every inch of outside skin on his tincan was, and he ducked and dived through the slenderest alleyways of traffic like some kind of animal ... In fact. that was it!, the tincan was an extension of himself and he was ducking and jiving like an Aboriginal Aussie rules football player. And when the opposition defence got too obstructive – four lanes of raggedy parked traffic at the red light, with bicycles and pedestrians all taking up any inch of space – he took off the road and went around that corner on a broad footpath! Hah! He did it all so effortlessly and with such clear-eyed athleticism that I just satta there and marvelled. I don't know how he didn't hit anybody or cause an accident, but he did it languorously, driving me home quicker and smoother than any other taxi-driving maniac in this crazy city.

>He REAL cool
>He no need no driving school
>He a crazy Zen driving fool
>Playing the road like he's shooting pool ...

RAW

my emotions are wheat ears
in a cornfield
China days spent
teaching not writing
smog rolling in
no air to breathe
dog fattened beneath my window
for the building team's
last supper on site –
'they're from the south' says a local

don't know what to believe anymore

China Big Bizness (double happiness)
doing backroom deals to buy
the West's favours
while taxi drivers have Mao dolls
with nodding heads
on their dashboards

As I fish for images
in the murky waters of Shanxi's Lethe
Fred whispers Camus –
'One must imagine Sisyphus happy.'

I'm a wheat ear in a cornfield
looking for favourable winds home.

THE NEXT POEM

There is a man who sits at the edge of the polluted pool
every morning when I put the kettle on and again in
the evening as I wash-up dishes and make a cup of tea.
All this evening there has been the droning sound of
a marital argument in Mandarin upstairs in
the Party Secretary's unit, and now the slamming of
this building's front door with its tricky locks. A moth
flies at the light as I enter the kitchen to make a late night
cup of tea. I'll use the earlier bag again. I talk
calmly to the moth but it has flown up into
the extractor fan's hood. No need for heroics, I say.
That's when the front door really slammed,
even though I put it in earlier in this poem, eager
to get the job underway, to find the next poem. And
form? I often hope to burst into flame, to
whistle forth a libretto or a fresh example of
exotica, as I sit here in tee-shirt and jeans, late night,
typing on a laptop, my back to the window where,
just perhaps - and I will turn around in just a moment
when I've finished typing this – where, perhaps,
the next poem sticks its tongue out at me and jeers
in any one of the world's many tongues,
Catch me if you can, catch me if you can.
There is a man who sits at the edge of the polluted pool
every morning and again in the evening. For all I know
he may be there right now, fishing in the dark, 11.38pm.

SHINING TO THE MISTY HILLS

Sakura Hotel in February
looking out our 13th floor window
Kunming shining to the misty hills
rooftops speckled with solar panels
dusty cactus in pots on window sills
glittery glass buildings
wet black bitumen ribbons
Dong Feng Dong Lu
advertising signs six storeys high
white chalk characters on pavement slabs
         before broken beggars
thin bent woman balancing a pole of
two bamboo baskets of bright red strawberries
    as the book-keeper
        balances his book

SPICE OF LIFE

wafting up
keyboard notes from
a crippled man flat on a wheel-bed
playing for his supper
on the walkover's deck

as we make love
on our hotel bed in
lazy afternoon sunshine
which falls through our
thirteenth floor window
in a sprinkling of motes.

Crossing the walkover later
for spinach dumplings,
I drop coins into his hat.
He responds with
'Sand shoe' as clear as day
between bars of days of
wine and roses.

TOOTLE LINGO

thirteen floors below us
contrapuntal traffic flows
in eight directions at once
(at least!) and bells on bikes tinkle
pitched above the beeping of scooters
beside honking horns of impatient taxis
and bullying bellicose trucks
challenging long-winded baritone buses
as the bullfrog-bassoon police wagon
pulls the Kunming Sinfonia into line
with an extended note *hooonk-hooonk*
and a mega-megaphonic order

HAPPY HOUR

Rock faces of Tai Bai Mountain
are stained with ink
Li Bai threw away in rage.

Now Adamson writes
of Mallarme's first drafts
as a squid squirts black ink in his boat –

meaning and faith are
two squirts of brain ink drying
on the wings of fantasy.

This page burns in autumn light.

I'm thinking this one out
behind bottles of Quink
lined up like cocktails on a bar.

GIBB RIVER RIPRAP

Solidity of bark, leaf, or wall
    riprap of things
    Gary Snyder

Out in the prickly yard
    first day of this stay
        at Gibb River Station
    in the red dust
of The Kimberley
    I hunt rocks to
        build a barbecue
    lifting and wheeling
brown rocks
    big and small
        to a burnt circle
    by the wire fence
interlopers on this landscape
    Jeanette wearing her
        Chinese 'Tree of Life' dress
    our lives riprapped together
        our histories
balanced precariously
    like these ragged rocks
        holes just right so evening breezes
can aerate   as Buddha said
    it is burning with birth

GIBB RIVER YACHT CLUB

Blue sails in the backyard
the fitted sheet billows
like a spinnaker
and the clothesline turns
on its centreplate.

I daydream of
an afternoon sailing
on the Swan River
and the cool of
a yacht club bar.

Two ibis fly off fence posts
a thirsty cow in
the sun-dried paddock
complains.

Black crows all tell her
there's no barman here
to serve a cold one
this mob all gone
to Derby Rodeo …

I shake my head,
unpeg the washing –
my wife's black knickers
start another line

NGALLAGUNDA USED CAR YARD

After the demolition derby
of time and neglect
motor bodies rust
in the long grass

I name it
The Ngallagunda Used Car Yard
the fruit of neglect
that runs down the road
and stops here
among poplar gums

Every community has one –
a dump for dead machinery
windows stowed in
bonnets up and twisted
exhaust pipes like
King Browns climbing down

Teenagers shelter inside
gunja smoke curling out
where a window once was

Wheels gone seats out
shell of
a Holden Commodore
from Bunbury
three thousand kilometres away
registration plates dangling

You can smell the rubber
on the highway as the cops chase
kids racing out of one life
into the next

NGALLAGUNDA GIRL

On my way to Wanalirri school this morning, taking the long track because of many snake trails heading into the bush near our shortcut, I saw a local girl of indeterminable age dancing on the road by herself, and watching her shadow, head tilted to one side checking to see she had the movements just right ...

Ngallagunda girl dances
seven years old
thin black body
silhouetted on
pindan track

Ngallagunda girl dances
songless and alone
head cocked left
watching her
undulating shadow
to get it right
to move like Mum

Ngallagunda girl dances
as little brother
plays muster
in the dirt where
king browns mated
under a full moon
their tracks lyrical in the sun

GROOVES

On hard rock ridges in The Kimberley –
red flushed cheekbones on an ancient face –
grooves scar the surface
where Jaru sharpened their spears.
Wild extremes of weather
haven't worn these stones flat,
millennia haven't erased the patina
of one civilisation before another,
the one before us now.

In my mind I feel grooves
of dogma, prayers and chants,
and the delicious incense
of candles snuffed after Benediction.
Torrential rains have questioned them,
wild winds proved weaker than their hold.
At night in the yard I stand, evaluating
their mark, their meaning,
and turn away
unsatisfied.

'The adventure novel of everyday life' MIKHAIL BAKHTIN

I wake to
one lyrical song,
the other a single bell

      frogs on late shift
      sleep now

            gecko holds fast on
            the window's flywire

      cotton sheets fall over
      my wife's reclining figure

one breast escapes
a nipple tests
the morning air

      by the bed I stand
      cock at half mast

            head in the interactive syntax of dream

~

on my upper arm,
a live branch in the tropical air,
a praying mantis
jumps, tree-leaf green
with fine limbs, two red
pinhead eyes on his
face, balanced above
praying hands on delicate arms,
enquiring now of the air,
of my body, of my pores.

                                      I stand
to escort him outdoors,
talking to him all the while,
watching his arms and head rise up further
as sound waves break over him, tongue
of this strange tree
        talking
        lovingly.

WATER COLOUR MORNING

The farm is in water colour this morning as the rain falls and rests on leaves and in puddles on firebreaks and tracks. Down the pebbly slope from the house, a burnt out tractor rusts faster for this wintry attention, a small pool where the farmer once sat. In the middle of the green paddock, fallow now since the last owner left with his paint brushes and easels, a kangaroo stands head held high, stock still in the rain, sniffing the wind. At first glance he could be mistaken for a tall stump of a burnt out tree – he's as grey as weathered timber and shadows on this overcast morning camouflage him like areas of burnt bark. His mob moves in the trees beyond the fence where the posts are dappled with lichen on the leeward side and raindrops hang from the wires like thousands of birds' eyes watching the sun struggle through grey clouds. Far in the distance, far beyond the township which is 17 kilometres away as the eagle flies, lies Geographe Bay. It can be seen in water colour from here on Chapman Hill, framed by the wide glass doors which open onto a raised wooden deck – kangaroo, tree plantation, distant paddocks with cattle, Busselton township, then the bay. Down in the right hand bottom corner, the artist's old studio sits like a scribbly signature, rough hewn timber planks for walls and rusting corrugated iron roof, bush path to its weathered door overgrown with brown rocks painted yellow on top to light a walker's way by moonlight. Because the putty has dried out, the glass of a window in the old studio falls and crashes to the cement floor, startling the roo in the field who bounds into the plantation, scaling the fence with one effortless leap.

THE BALLAD OF MANY CROWS

As I sat out upon a hill
Upon a hill, upon a hill
I looked up at the crows that fill
The leafy trees of Wagga

I saw their eyes like marbles black
Like marbles black, like marbles black
And felt a chill run down my back
Beneath the trees of Wagga

A woman there had told a tale
She told a tale, she told a tale
How the town had felt five years' betrayal
Since crows returned to Wagga

"Our men have heard the crows' sad song
The crows' sad song, the crows' sad song
Until by their own hand they've gone —
I curse the crows of Wagga"

Farmers are a steady lot, not given much to fancy
Born to heed the call to be as iron tough as Clancy

Now they hang themselves in their dark loss
In their dark loss, in their dark loss
When the crows' stark song becomes their cross
Among the trees of Wagga

Black-eyed and beaky with a mourning cry
A mourning cry, a mourning cry
Crows trespass and fly
To cast their eye on Wagga.

Now's the time to break the spell
To break the spell, to break the spell
To greet the future and fare well
Among the trees of Wagga

I go inside to write my song
To write my song, to write my song
The crows know nought of right and wrong
In the leafy trees of Wagga

from *One Hour Seeds Another*

THE BEST TEACHER

The cat fidgets on the parapet
facing the roof next door
testing her nerve against
the chasm between.
Floodlit by morning sun
she stands, and sits, and whips
her tail, and partly sits but
stands again, and – just as
I write her fright – she leaps.
Plonk. All four on roof tiles.
It wasn't so far. Now
she digs along the gutter,
looking for dead lizards
and such easy prey. A brave heart
on an autumn day. I've been
fidgeting for days, getting up
and down, brewing tea, forgetting
tea, opening files, reading
old poems and emails. Now
that I'm here, it wasn't so far.

THE NAME OF THE GAME

Oh, I see, it is the time
of year for lace faced fungus,
woodlice and red-bellied ants, snails
that deckle our mail, and the trimming
of our curry tree.

In the shallow pond
across the road a white-faced heron
looks for frogs and freshwater snails
grateful for anything in this muddy water.
We walk by,

dogs sniffing the news,
looking where new growth
grows green and bright from the late
summer bushfire. It looks so fresh against
charred trunks.

In dried edges
of the pond, before its
low banks, the council tried
a re-vegetation program at the end
of summer, but

the heat hung on,
and now we see the few
survivors dusted off by late
autumn rain. I straighten bamboo
to prop up

new plants. Last year
and the year before that
we did the same – small areas
of fledgling trees and bushes
supporting each other.

Perseverance is
the name of the game,
returning to earth what
is the earth's for the Planet Earth
to be continued.

NOTEBOOK "singing they sang"

    singing they sang
    one, two ... then paused
    only to sing in rhythm
    one, two, three, four
        feet stomping the floor
            give peace a chance
            give peace a chance
    I remember before them
    listening to Tom Paxton
    singing he sang
        peace in the world
        or the world in pieces
    pointing his plectrum at
    all fascists

    ~

    then there was our local man
    who put a CD player
    into the polished trunk of a tree –
        he didn't hear the tree
                singing
            a different suite song
        for every season ...

    a dove in a she-oak
    listens as I write
    a small sparrow
        chirps and titters
    in a red nut bush –

     text in the context
song from the nest

~

on the road to Gundagai
cows lunch by
the rest area ...

riding a Greyhound bus
I think of Kerouac and co
         in this sparse
Australian landscape on
an air-conditioned coach

reading AA recovery stories
socking water back

writing now with
a Tasmanian Poetry Festival pen
chitter-chatter from
Chinese girls behind me

transcendental clouds
   differ day to day
they sit above
gentle hillocks
like meditating sheep

~

      small timber cottage
          among ancestors
      untrimmed

      old man at the gate
          likewise

~

      leaf green differs as
      seasons move on

Vivaldi's four seasons
not native here

here they count six
in this land full
of extremes
deserts and flood plains
snow falls and droughts

SITTING ON THE FRONT PERCH

sitting on the front perch
listening to gentle spring rain
a bird small as a newborn's fist
anonymous in grey and white
tweets in rich green foliage
of a magnolia tree
tweets merrily
non-stop to the universe

rain falls heavier
but she keeps tweeting
mailman comes along on his little scooter
pumping exhaust fumes out
into the rain-washed air
stops at our gate
drops litter into our box
little anon looks on
silent
until the machine rolls on
and with it
the Yellow-crested Mailbird

NOTEBOOK (Darlington)

Ganesha burns among
milk cartons   plastic coke bottles
cockroaches

in a cold
hillside morning
a boy repeats his callsign
          endlessly

frog replies

ceremonies together

ants run across my thought
~
beside Highway 1
grey fur
moves among dry
lantana –
doe rabbit
hunts and gathers
while above
fat butcherbird
throws
his weight around
in the little birds' nest
I worry for them
mind leaving the page
Celestial Tea gone cold

LATE WINTER NIGHT

The old dog is snoring. It's a comforting sound late night in this empty house. The gas heater has warmed the furniture, walls, carpets and floorboards, and the dishwasher in the kitchen has filed away my sparse dishes for washing with tomorrow's lot.

This poem has no birds in it, as Jack Spicer said some time off. I've been reading him, there's nothing on TV. It is late in this dry winter and at last the earth here is wet with rain. Three ducks from the rising waters of the swamp waddle for dinner across our overgrown and weed-filled lawn. They are silent and not in this poem.

I turn ABC Jazz off and the dog stops snoring. Is there any meaning in this? The day is interlaced with such relationships yet we drudge through our hours, aware of insignificance. I often think of reality as a knitting pattern with multiple dimensions, knit one, purl two. No pattern, just chaos and its resultant energy.

Her snoring returns as I rise to turn off the heater and get ready to go to bed. I stand beside her, looking down for a moment before she wakes, yawns, and looks at me questioningly. *I don't know*, I tell her, *I don't know either*.

ON THE VERGE

out early
watering the roses
before sunrise

I scratch my neck
and dislodge a bee

drunk already

~

next week's
council pick-up
has grown a fair crop

fringing the road
on browning grass

white goods
stained lounges

broken bikes and
office chairs that don't
hold office anymore

~

when evening falls
young boys
punch the shit out of
the washing machine
which once washed
their nappies

leaving the white pedestal
standing
      arse up

~

all creatures have
Buddha-nature

except bored boys*

(*with apologies to Gary Snyder)

COUNTING THE BEADS

> *The rosary beads you gave me*
> *A quarter of a century ago*
> *I found again last night.*
> *Still an unbeliever, I fondle*
> *These beads and our ritual past.*
>   Epistle to Andrew *Viv Kitson*

Morning after morning
we filed into the chapel
and knelt. I rubbed my beads,
counting off prayers, worrying
about maths equations and verbatim
renditions of old poems. A gaunt
Christ hung welded to a copper cross
above a sharp-angled altar conflicting with
the school's old Stations of the Cross
rehung on salmon brick walls:
a betrayal, a crucifiction. After
Rosary we filed out in pairs.

Now poems are my prayers
lifting off book pages, my new words
wriggling like pupae between
ruled lines.
              Poet, friend,
sometimes I dream of us sitting as
elder tribesmen in the desert between
Sydney and Perth, sharing a poem a bead,
calling the spirits up.

IF THE WORLD IS THOUGHT
i.m. Viv Kitson

doves dine on
last night's rice

such little things
make a life

make me realize
you're not here

*

                remembering
our flat just up
                from Mosman jetty
home of a mad dog
                running around the yard
jumping up at the quarry face
jumping up
and jumping up at the quarry face

            where Buddha sat
            in an alcove

Sydney '62
the Rosicrucian lady upstairs
with an ancient face
a young woman body
convinced me
the world is thought

I've thought it ever since

*

A strange incident in the hospital: I was wheeled down to the charge nurse in the X-ray unit for admission and she leaned over me and said: "Who wrote these lines – 'Jazz at the El Rocco and rats at Circular Quai'?" A rather bizarre moment, given the circumstances! After the initial shock, I replied: "I did. But I wrote them when I was 20." Charge nurse turned out to be N.... B.... who started 1st year uni just as I was completing my last. She apparently came to some reading you and I organised (did we?) and is a friend of T.... H....'s. Don't know if you recall her.

I'll have to go now. I have to email my sister to discuss how we break my cancer news to Mum. Then I'll have to phone my sister-in-law tomorrow for ditto. In fact, after nearly a fortnight in hospital, there are a lot of things to sort out...

Love,

Viv

*

your wife blames
your body for
your death –
she said
We're cremating the body today
her tone accusatory

she has a point
your body
your ship
your horse
your house
your cave
your clubhouse
your friend
your lightning rod

*

if the world is thought
and you are gone
has someone stopped
thinking of you?

CHAINMAN IN SUMMER

The Perth to Kalgoorlie pipeline
is a never-ending story
on a brittle landscape. If
you put your ear to it, its chill
enters your mind and you imagine
you hear water. You hear water.
Invariably the sun blazes down
and all is untouchably hot –
road bitumen sticks to your boots
and the horizon wavers in
the rippling air. In the survey team
of the Main Roads Department
we mark the way with white dots
measured to fall central to the trail
mapped by theodolite and equations
on graph paper. We finish a bottle
of beer, laughingly called a King Brown
around here, then walk up the road
a stretch, and place the empty central
on a rise. Such is the topography
of dot painting, chainman style.

The birds are still in flight. Believe the birds. ~
JACK SPICER

    Tuesday morning, 10.45am, Northbridge is dead.
    The Deen, partiest pub on a Saturday night,
    is a silent, empty shell. A Chinese youth
    cleans down the window ledges
    and door entrances – scrubbing,
    rinsing, pushing sudsy water to the gutter.
    The weekend news on television
    and the front pages of the press
    are often filled with images
    of this pub's brawling patrons and
    forensic close-ups of dried pools of blood.
    Now, all is silent, except a light chirping,
    a skipping note whistled from
    a tiny beak. I look up at the top windows
    and the old awning fixtures long disused.
    There a small finch hops and darts
    delightedly between perches, hop, dart,
    tweet, a single note whistled
    over and over like she is singing
    to herself, imagining a new nest
    and little ones within it,
    tiny beaks tweeting in
    morning sunlight.

ANAESTHETICS

I enter, not knowing who
I'm going to see :: dead, living,
actors slipping into their roles
for theatre. I greet all I meet
with a face reflecting
the intelligence of a decorated biscuit
at a birthday party. Down
long corridors of light, I'm facing
her face and his face, upside down,
clowns taking me for a ride. They
stop and shift me to a serving tray.
Soon I am floating in liquid air
where I keep my true self, mid-deep
in a lake where naught swim but I.
I am their balloon to pump, then
pop with their sharp knives.
I surface to play my role, an impro
where parts are tagged and we
create our own diurnal dialogues
and midnight monologues to those
playing torchlight nurse. My balloon self
sags in a field where the tent is up, a circus
of before nows, yesterdays, and dead ones
who have stayed for one reason or
no other. Once they circled, smiling
as they came into focus before
their skin flaked off and blew away
in a silent breeze. Again I am
in their hands, again I float from
their theatre to my circus domain –
now my mother approaches

with a friendly grin made all
the more horrific by her death. It isn't
about her – it's about me. Yet
I still don't understand, as I return
with my laughing biscuit intelligence
fresh from the baking fire.

UNDER A BLACK BERET

I put on my black corduroy French beret
listen to Brad Mehldau Trio
read manifestoes of various poetry schools
click to the rhythm on my keyboard
like once I did on the table at El Rocco
so young back then my fingers never tired
smile at the memory of my first poems
their cheap wine flavour
so (now) put the pot on to brew
black coffee always black coffee
the whole image revolved around black coffee
even when still in my school suit
ordering *café noir*, please at El Calib
or late night at The Coffee Pot
where they'd put on *Oscar Peterson plays
Porgy & Bess* when I walked in…
I'm sitting here late night decades later
arthritis slowing my knuckles
Brad Mehldau Trio on *Spotify*

another full moon
blown out
old dog asleep on the couch
snoring in
our air-conditioned air

SELF PORTRAIT, WITH BEE

In all this long back garden of vegetables
and blossoming roses, a fat healthy thistle grows
sturdy, spiky and green. Atop one
of three green bulbs on reaching stalks, a colour
bursts through, a colour like light purple or dark pink –
a first blossom among the green. It is so vibrant
in this autumn sunlight it attracts a bee
who lands and buzzes, turns around
to another angle and buzzes again, and repeats
this manoeuvre a few times, specifically three,
then flies off. I am standing here, watching,
as my wife talks about what we should do
to the garden, how the cat over the fence
is fouling our vegetable patch and not covering
its own shit well enough. *Wow, I say, wow,
look at this.* And she turns to see me fascinated
with a thistle bush and its attendant bee.
Yes, I left it there, she comments, *I know
the funny things you like, thistles and things.*

THE OTHER WOMAN

Nina Simone died yesterday. The café girl
told me when I asked, 'That's nice . Who's on piano?'
'Nina Simone,' she said. 'She died today.'
I stopped and stood, confused. 'That's what happened
to me when I heard,' the girl said. I smiled, 'But she,
she's been around ...' I tumbled over words
to teenage nights, girl on my lap, lights
low, Nina on the stereo. My sweet
affair lasted months – Nina and I,
forty plus years. Dead at seventy in her home
in France. Now jazz jockeys play 'Nina at Newport'.
A record company has a tribute ready. It's a long time
since that girl was in my lap. We had lunch
last Thursday. I didn't hear what was playing.

LOVE, OH LOVE, OH CARELESS LOVE

"Above the giant funhouse and the ghosts
I hear the seagulls call."
                              – Jack Spicer

Once there was a setting, ocean side,
moonlit waves, yes, but it has
gone now. There was a girl,
yes, Burmese Irish, but she too
has gone. The waves wash up
and down the beach, but I'm no
longer there. Her breasts
rise in my hands as seagulls call.
We wait to order burgers
above the beach from a van parked
on salty grass – Van Eileen. One joke
too many, although I have learnt since
laughter has its place in intimacy. Yes,
Eileen too has gone. A tourist webcam
on Cottesloe Beach shows car parking
wherever waves don't wash. 'Salt?'
'No thanks, there's plenty here
already.' She laughs and he puts
out his hand for cash. The story
is my thing now, yes, but somewhere
she is real, breasts heavier, thighs
thicker, no beach sand between toes,
an orchardist's wife – or should I say,
an orchardist. That's another thing:
gender relationships have changed
since then. Yet, she stays with me still
in my bookshelves under Tagore,
a collection dedicated to
My favourite library in her convent hand.

SHE WAITS FOR ME
for Jeanette

she waits for me
as I do my washing
porridge on the stove

when we marry
we will have
more grandchildren

it is our 'last true love'
we say, gazing at each other
like herons on river rocks

I bring my porridge
to the table
and think in its steam –

too much cinnamon
and not enough
metaphor

I REMEMBER LUCAS
i.m. Lucas North 19??-2012

On a hot summer's day
on the driveway of Tom Collins House,
near the path up Melon Hill, an old stained
VW Beetle stood like a wreck awaiting the final ball,
tattooed by time, loved for its every spluttering mile.
The bonnet was up, Lucas was tinkering
and we were talking away, away
from literary gossip, away from farm work's
lonesome nights in the bush. We talked
against the built-in obsolescence of
modern manufacturing, we shared
the sentimentality we had for old things –
cars, his skateboards, my manual typewriters.

Inside Tom Collins House, Lucas
built and set a possum trap.
He could turn a hand
to more than words, he could
turn an ankle to skateboarding, too.
Where's he gone now
to tinker and build? Where
is he setting his next narrative?
Now, skaters at the suburban park
leave a space as they hurtle and turn,
police scan traffic
for the patchwork Vee-dub,
and I smile at the possum stain
in our old back shed and think
of Lucas tinkering away.

ABSENCE

Since you've been
gone I've been
on retreat, so
to speak.
Now a gunshot
echoes through the
still morning air.
Corellas scatter.
My Mingus morning
bothers no-one. It
heightens the silence that
wraps itself around these
empty rooms. Piano
trills run through
my breakfast steam
as our dog sits
where your feet
should be. You
left the camera
behind – I won't take
photos of things
you know so well.
The flautist plays
with tambourines
on his feet to
embellish the beat,
as you wear

that chunky neck-
lace to lift
your heart. A
white cabbage moth
flies to the window
and calls us out.
I open the gate
and look down
the road.

ANEURYSM

At 81 my mother asked for a cigarette
from the nurses' station. They were
her cigarettes, monitored by the home.
She lit up, said she didn't feel too good, and
went to the toilet. Her cigarette lay
in a tray. She came out, shuffling
in her fur-edged slippers down the hall
and fell straight on her face. Fellow
inmates held back, a nurse ran forward.
She had died before she hit the carpet,
her mouth open and surprise
in her eyes. Where she
had gone was anybody's guess.
A priest arrived before her doctor,
a fact interpreted differently
by family and management.

XPT SYDNEY TO MELBOURNE

sitting at Central
        rock cake   cappuccino
6.35am   for breakfast
        long grey beards
in preponderance
        one carries a long tube
wrapped in its own   sleeping bag
two eagle feathers   flying   from its grip
        didgeridoo   ceremonial
not for busking
        other greybeard's guitar   open to
            the weather 'as to grief'
all music   seasonal   ceremonial
        this train   a rhythm section
woodwinds outside   silent   behind glass
        XTP rhythm section   regular
        as kangaroos

as I throw my rubbish in the cafeteria's bin
I see another bushy grey beard
        'I once had a beard like yours,' I say
in my gregarious way – his beard flows
        salt and pepper   from his suntanned cheeks
luxurious as they say   he looks at
        my tightly clipped tidy beard
'Wot appened   ya get married?'

on Brett Whiteley's studio wall
        'death is better than   249 NA meetings'
everything in excess   to escape   trapped
        'wisdom to know the difference'

Chinese girl in First Class   writes   simple characters
        in her notebook   beautiful calligraphy
with an everyday biro   line by beautiful line
      I praise her   but she doesn't hear me
earbuds in   listening to Beyoncé

now   down the thin aisle   staggers
       a fat man   big   bulbous
lucky to fit between the seats   sweaty tee-shirt
      unable to hide his girth   REBEL
                    Metallica
    his wild grey beard flies above

our service today is fully booked ...

as I weave to the buffet car
      jagged sculptural forms
          of passengers asleep
by our track   poplars standing leafless   clickety clack
ah   up and down the aisle   jean clad
     legs bums and crotches   scissor
way back   there were no jeans
      in my teenage years
      just workingmen's denim trousers
we bought them under the influence of Beat lit
     cut leather belts shorter   to fit
juvenile hips
             now even the oldies wear them
they wear them with
      the dust of cattleyards   shearing shed
      washed out of their tough hides

~

30 year old man   bald with a ginger beard
         wearing army fatigues   soaks up the sun
         weathered ankles
         wiggling ginger-haired toes
a long way from war

he reads essays George Orwell wrote with his bare
hands

~

I scoff at the lady   over the aisle   who paid
         too much for *The Australian Women's Weekly*
as I open my *Paris Review* $25 from Gleebooks

beware throwing stones

~

she is tiny
         white haired and tidy
as a polished kettle

now she wants to pick up
         her cardboard tray   issued one per traveller
fallen to the floor beneath her feet   she stretches
         and misses   so she pushes the tray
with her right foot (sensibly shod)   until her left hand
                              can reach it –

         'ah' she says   and sits back   comfortable

I notice her Persil white socks

~
a bespectacled gentleman   in tidy casual
       reads   *Enlightened Leadership*
too late?
~

"Like a body with bone and flesh a poem needs different densities."
Henri Cole *Paris Review 209*

LOCAL LANGUAGE

Dog pisses on the cracks. De Saussure
said as much: Sign is a signifier.
We drive up the black highway,
reading the language of short signs
and translating the body language
of roadkill. The council writes its code
in spring yellow. Esoteric knowledge
creates them and us. Who writes has a plan:
who executes has a duty. This old town
has its own babble and squeak, from
the foul smell of the piggery up one end
to the sweet smell of processed oats
up the other.

NOTEBOOK: CAFE POEM

Waitress with
    a happy face
delivers a 'large Cap'
      while my head
          is down as
I write in this pad.
"Are you waiting on
      anything else?"
I look up.
    "Just inspiration."
She takes a step
    back and
shakes it all about.
    Stops. Shrugs.
"That's all I've got ..."

I write her down, inspired

MOODY REQUIEM

each breath a beat to
begin the moody requiem

the light pizzicato toward
a tympani climax

I hear it tick
a steady four/four

when I walk the dog -
then skip a beat

wake me in
pitch black of night –

the pipes travel
their new routes

as the organ pumps
the remaining blues

THE WHEELIE BIN NOVEL

As domestic duty would have it
I went outside with the recyclable rubbish,
staring down at how many newspapers,
cereal boxes, tissues and cosmetic containers
we chuck out – and all the words with them.
There's a good novel in there, I thought, as I threw more
into the wheelie bin – nouns, adjectives, adverbs,
prepositions, conjunctions, weights and measures,
imperial and decimal. It's a variety show or
a beehive of human communications, mixed up
with a denouement – a dollop of yoghurt
and some dregs of wine.

REVERSE HAIBUN

measuring the step
with her chin –
blind dog.

~

My dog wants an appearance fee
for yesterday's haiku. Okay, I say,
and give her a *Smacko* (Beef).
Not good enough, she wants two.
No way! Think of your weight!
But dogs think in the present tense,
no future worries. To avoid
contractual headaches, I stop
writing about her. She humphs
and goes through her doggy door
to tell the moon her grievances.

PAPER TALES

Closely typed and printed pages of
an academic draft lie in the basket

screwed up and thrown higgledy-piggledy
screaming of frustration and anger.

Beneath lies the flat and restrained
text of a child's self-penned story

first draft in her own hand. I pour
my breakfast tea and ponder how

a recycling basket can say so much,
little sculptures expressing the mood

of their sculptor, how paper
speaks of the trees it came from.

AT WOOLIES' CARPARK

'You drive like a poet,' his wife said,
and he's puzzled over it for weeks.
When he drives straight down the highway
is it a run-on sentence, only end-stopped
at the town's traffic lights? Thinking about it
he pulls into Woolies' carpark next to
another small Toyota and forms
a rhyming couplet. When he says
'aubergine' for 'eggplant', she scowls,
so he answers before she can criticise,
'I simply like the sound of it –
oh-bur-jean. Nice.' She walks on,
he pushes the wobbly trolley
and tracks left to right like
Ricciardo warming his tyres.
She hisses, 'What *are* you doing?!'
And he smiles, 'I'm a free verse poet,
No curbs here!' She turns and walks off.

PLAYING A 500 YEAR-OLD OAK

With a burst and rush
of salvage balloons
the drowned oak trunk
breaks water
like a sheet of silence …
On dry land
an instrument maker
taps with a knuckle
and his knock ripples back
through circles which sank
and lay waiting to be scored,
fences strung to play
knotty fence lines
before violinists.
In the oak's ringed ripples
mill hands dance on logs,
fiddlers play tides of wood
and working songs of
loggers who fell the trees,
saws singing and swinging axes
beside the log-jammed waterways,
in sweet scent of sap, blossom of air,
knotty notes, sweat rivering
down lumberjacks' backs,
sunlight falling like planks
throughout the forest.

Envoi

Rack upon rack
of violins
hung up to dry

sap running
down their bodies
like birth sheen.

ECHIDNA CROSSING

Driving in the moonless dark, passing the overgrown Toodyay racetrack opposite where the caravan park forlornly sits, my headlights pick up a stone on the road, a stone that moves – a dome with hair atop like an American sailor in port, spiky.

I stop, he stops. Impasse. He is rolled up tight, his bristles straight up catching high beam. I switch the lights down to normal and whisper, 'Come on, mate, off the road.'

He lies doggo, paralysed by stage fright. Trees sway, a thin moon peeks out between storm clouds. 'I can't stay here all night' – but I know I will rather than hurt him.

For a townie like me Echidna is a name from children's storybooks – this bitumen showcase is no place to meet.

I'm musing on the word echidna when he moves on in a very slow waddle, forward, tentatively .

I'm tempted to applaud, to yell encouragement – 'Aussie, Aussie, Aussie – Oi!Oi! Oi!' – but I sit and watch silently. He's no Cathy Freeman. He circles back the way he came. There's more road that way, it doesn't make sense, but he's the echidna, I'm just the lighting technician. He walks; pauses; walks.

So I am released to go on my way. I notice high winds have taken down the 'Echidna Crossing' sign up Stirlingia Road. I hadn't believed it until now.

SPRING SILENCE

Piano notes, a blow fly
and bees buzzing. *May I
humbly ask you not to speak?*
In this old country house
the woodwork remembers
wind, nostalgia in every knot.

Floor, chairs and table,
doors and jambs, sideboard,
window and picture frames,
residual wind hums beneath
neighbourhood noises.
A day without a clanger in my bell,
I hear the sweet song
of everything else.

AFTERNOON TEA

Memory is the mothership.
I wash and rinse pots and pans,
remembering the scraggly tall
European refugees working
in the kitchen of the boarding school
I went to in the Fifties. I can't
remember ever knowing their names
yet here they work, crusty aprons on
and giant silver trays glinting
as they walk toward the spreading tree
where we queue in the shade, hungry
as growing boys can be, and take
one gigantic slice of fresh baked bread
spread with strawberry jam. Ah,
that jam!

www.ingramcontent.com/pod-product-compliance
Lightning Source LLC
Chambersburg PA
CBHW021023110526
R18276100001B/R182761PG44588CBX00013B/23